DEPARTMENT OF ENERGY

Energy Conservation Program for Consumer Products: Energy Conservation Standards for Hearth Products

AGENCY: Office of Energy Efficiency and Renewable Energy, Department of Energy.

ACTION: Notice of proposed rulemaking and announcement of public meeting.

SUMMARY: The Energy Policy and Conservation Act of 1975 (EPCA), as amended, sets forth various provisions designed to improve energy efficiency for consumer products and certain commercial and industrial equipment. In addition to specifying a list of covered residential products and commercial equipment, EPCA contains provisions that enable the Secretary of Energy to classify additional types of consumer products as covered products. The U.S. Department of Energy (DOE) has previously published a proposed determination of coverage to classify gas-fired hearth products as covered consumer products under the applicable provisions in EPCA. In this document, DOE proposes an energy conservation standard for hearth products following its notice of

1

proposed coverage determination. This proposed rule also announces a public meeting to receive comment on the proposed standard and associated analyses and results.

DATES: <u>Meeting</u>: DOE will hold a public meeting on Wednesday, March 4, 2015, from 9:00 a.m. to 4:00 p.m., in Washington, DC. The meeting will also be broadcast as a webinar. See section VII, "Public Participation," for webinar registration information, participant instructions, and information about the capabilities available to webinar participants.

<u>Comments</u>: DOE will accept comments, data, and information regarding this notice of proposed rulemaking (NOPR) before and after the public meeting, but no later than **[INSERT DATE 60 DAYS AFTER DATE OF PUBLICATION IN THE FEDERAL REGISTER]**. See section VII, "Public Participation," for details.

ADDRESSES: The public meeting will be held at the U.S. Department of Energy, Forrestal Building, Room 8E-089, 1000 Independence Avenue, SW., Washington, DC 20585. To attend, please notify Ms. Brenda Edwards at (202) 586–2945. Please note that foreign nationals visiting DOE Headquarters are subject to advance security screening procedures. Any foreign national wishing to participate in the meeting should advise DOE as soon as possible by contacting Ms. Edwards at the phone number above to initiate the necessary procedures. Please also note that any person wishing to bring a laptop computer or tablet into the Forrestal Building will be required to obtain a property pass. Visitors should avoid bringing laptops, or allow an extra 45 minutes. Persons may also attend the public meeting via webinar. For more information, refer to section VII, "Public Participation," near the end of this notice.

Instructions: Any comments submitted must identify the NOPR for Energy Conservation Standards for Hearth Products, and provide docket number EERE-2014-BT-STD-0036 and/or regulatory information number (RIN) number 1904–AD35. Comments may be submitted using any of the following methods:

1. Federal eRulemaking Portal: www.regulations.gov. Follow the instructions for submitting comments.

2. E-mail: HearthHeatingProd2014STD0036@ee.doe.gov. Include the docket number and/or RIN in the subject line of the message. Submit electronic comments in Word Perfect, Microsoft Word, PDF, or ASCII file format, and avoid the use of special characters or any form on encryption.

3. Postal Mail: Ms. Brenda Edwards, U.S. Department of Energy, Building Technologies Office, Mailstop EE-5B, 1000 Independence Avenue, SW., Washington, DC, 20585-0121. If possible, please submit all items on a compact disc (CD), in which case it is not necessary to include printed copies.

4. Hand Delivery/Courier: Ms. Brenda Edwards, U.S. Department of Energy, Building Technologies Office, 950 L'Enfant Plaza, SW., Suite 600, Washington, DC, 20024. Telephone: (202) 586-2945. If possible, please submit all items on a CD, in which case it is not necessary to include printed copies.

Written comments regarding the burden-hour estimates or other aspects of the collection-of-information requirements contained in this proposed rule may be submitted to Office of Energy Efficiency and Renewable Energy through the methods listed above and by e-mail to Chad_S_Whiteman@omb.eop.gov.

No telefacsimilies (faxes) will be accepted. For detailed instructions on submitting comments and additional information on the rulemaking process, see section VII of this document (Public Participation).

Docket: The docket, which will include all relevant Federal Register notices, public meeting attendee lists and transcripts, comments, and other supporting documents/materials, is available for review at www.regulations.gov. All documents in the docket are listed in the www.regulations.gov index. However, some documents listed in the index may not be publically available, such as those containing information that is exempt from public disclosure.

A link to the docket webpage can be found at: http://www1.eere.energy.gov/buildings/appliance_standards/rulemaking.aspx?ruleid=84 . This webpage contains a link to the docket for this notice on the www.regulations.gov site. The www.regulations.gov webpage contains simple instructions on how to access all documents, including public comments, in the docket. See section VII, "Public Participation," for further information on how to submit comments through www.regulations.gov.

For further information on how to submit a comment, review other public comments and the docket, or participate in the public meeting, contact Ms. Brenda Edwards at (202) 586-2945 or by email: Brenda.Edwards@ee.doe.gov.

FOR FURTHER INFORMATION CONTACT:

Mr. John Cymbalsky, U.S. Department of Energy, Office of Energy Efficiency and Renewable Energy, Building Technologies Office, EE-5B, 1000 Independence Avenue, SW., Washington, DC, 20585-0121. Telephone: (202) 287-1692. E-mail: HearthHeatingProd2014STD0036@ee.doe.gov.

Mr. Eric Stas, U.S. Department of Energy, Office of the General Counsel, GC-71, 1000 Independence Avenue, SW., Washington, DC 20585-0121. Telephone: (202) 586-9507. E-mail: Eric.Stas@hq.doe.gov.

For information on how to submit or review public comments, contact Ms. Brenda Edwards at (202) 586-2945 or by email: Brenda.Edwards@ee.doe.gov.

SUPPLEMENTARY INFORMATION:

Table of Contents

I. Summary of the Proposed Rule

Title III, Part B[1] of the Energy Policy and Conservation Act of 1975 (EPCA or

the Act), Pub. L. 94-163 (42 U.S.C. 6291-6309, as codified), established the Energy

Conservation Program for Consumer Products Other Than Automobiles.[2] In addition to

specifying a list of covered residential products and commercial equipment, EPCA

contains provisions that enable the Secretary of Energy to classify additional types of

consumer products as covered products. (42 U.S.C. 6292(a)(20)) In a proposed

---

[1] For editorial reasons, upon codification in the U.S. Code, Part B was redesignated Part A.
[2] All references to EPCA in this document refer to the statute as amended through the American Energy
Manufacturing Technical Corrections Act (AEMTCA), Pub. L. 112-210 (Dec. 18, 2012).

determination of coverage published in the Federal Register on December 31, 2013, DOE

proposed to classify hearth products as covered consumer products under EPCA. 78 FR

79638.

Pursuant to EPCA, any new or amended energy conservation standard must be

designed to achieve the maximum improvement in energy efficiency that is

technologically feasible and economically justified. (42 U.S.C. 6295(o)(2)(A))

Furthermore, the new or amended standard must result in a significant conservation of

energy. (42 U.S.C. 6295(o)(3)(B)) The statute also provides that not later than 6 years

after issuance of any final rule establishing or amending a standard, DOE must publish

either a notice of determination that standards for the product do not need to be amended,

or a notice of proposed rulemaking including new proposed energy conservation

standards. (42 U.S.C. 6295(m)(1))

In accordance with these and other statutory provisions discussed in this notice,

DOE proposes a new energy conservation standard for hearth products. The proposed

standard is a prescriptive design requirement for standby mode operation that would

disallow the use of continuously-burning pilots (i.e., "standing pilots" or "constant-

burning pilots") in hearth products. The proposed standard, if adopted, would apply to all

hearth products, as defined in section IV.A, that are manufactured in, or imported into,

the United States on and after the date 5 years after the publication of the final rule for

this rulemaking. The proposed design standard would eliminate all standby mode gas

consumption for hearth products as defined in the proposed determination rulemaking (78

FR 79638). DOE considered a combination of factors in developing its proposal to disallow continuously burning pilot lights, rather than other possibilities such as proposing to regulate active mode energy consumption with a performance standard or other prescriptive requirements. The rationale for this tentative decision to focus on standby mode energy consumption by the standing pilot is further explained in section III.B of this NOPR.

A. Benefits and Costs to Consumers

Table I.1 presents DOE's evaluation of the economic impacts of the proposed standard on consumers of hearth products, as measured by the average life-cycle cost (LCC) savings and the simple payback period (PBP).[3] The average LCC savings to consumers are positive and estimated at $165 over the lifetime of the average hearth product, and the PBP is estimated at 2.9 years, which is below the average hearth product lifetime of approximately 15 years.[4] As noted above, these impacts result from the removal of a continuously-burning pilot in units that would otherwise have them, which reduces the standby mode fossil fuel energy consumption of hearth products.[5]

---

[3] The average LCC savings are measured relative to the base-case efficiency distribution, which depicts the hearth product market in the compliance year (see section III.H). The simple PBP, which is designed to compare specific hearth product efficiency levels, is measured relative to the baseline (see section IV.C.1).
[4] See section IV.F.2.d for the derivation of the average hearth product lifetime.
[5] Impacts of match-lit hearth products were not included in the analysis. For more details, see section IV.A.1.

Table I.1 Impacts of Proposed Hearth Product Energy Conservation Standard on Consumers of Hearth Products

Product	Simple Average LCC Savings 2013$	Simple Payback Period years
Hearth Products	165	2.9

B. Impact on Manufacturers

The industry net present value (INPV) is the sum of the discounted cash flows for the industry from the base year through the end of the analysis period (2014 to 2050). Using a real discount rate of 8.7 percent, DOE estimates that the base case INPV for manufacturers of gas hearth products is $125.3 million in 2013$.[6] Under the proposed design standard, DOE expects that INPV impacts may range from a loss of 2.6 percent of INPV to a gain of 0.4 percent.

C. National Benefits and Costs

DOE's analyses indicate that the proposed energy conservation standard for hearth products would save a significant amount of energy in the form of reduced natural gas consumption during stand-by mode. The lifetime energy savings for hearth products purchased in the 30-year period that begins in the first full year of compliance with an amended standard (2021–2050), relative to the base case without amended standards, amount to 0.69 quads[7] of full-fuel-cycle (FFC) energy.[8] This represents a savings of

---

[6] All monetary values in this document are expressed in 2013 dollars; discounted values are discounted to 2014 unless explicitly stated otherwise.
[7] A quad is equal to 10^{15} British thermal units (Btu).
[8] The reported savings are net savings after accounting for the slight increase in electricity use resulting from the proposed standard.

about 77 percent relative to the energy use of the hearth product ignition systems in the base case, which reflects the existing market share of electronic ignition systems.

The cumulative net present value (NPV) of total consumer costs and savings for the proposed hearth products standard ranges from $1.03 billion to $3.12 billion at 7-percent and 3-percent discount rates, respectively. This NPV expresses the estimated total value of future operating-cost savings minus the estimated increased product costs for hearth products purchased in 2021–2050.

In addition, the proposed hearth products standard would have significant environmental benefits. The energy savings described above are expected to result in cumulative emission reductions of 37.0 million metric tons (Mt)[9] of carbon dioxide (CO_2), 486 thousand tons of methane (CH_4), 125 thousand tons of nitrogen oxides (NO_X), and 0.01 thousand tons of nitrous oxide (N_2O).[10] Projected emissions show an increase of 4.26 thousand tons of sulfur dioxide (SO_2) and 0.01 tons of mercury (Hg) due to higher electricity use associated with the shift to electronic ignition in the subject hearth products.[11] The cumulative reduction in CO_2 emissions through 2030 amounts to 11.1

---

[9] A metric ton is equivalent to 1.1 short tons. Results for emissions other than CO_2 are presented in short tons.

[10] The emissions reductions primarily concern reduction in combustion emissions from standing pilots. DOE calculated emissions reductions relative to the Annual Energy Outlook 2014 (AEO 2014) Reference case, which generally represents current legislation and environmental regulations, including recent government actions for which implementing regulations were available as of October 31, 2013. The impacts on mercury emissions are expected to be negligible.

[11] DOE calculated power sector emissions impacts relative to the Annual Energy Outlook 2014 (AEO 2014) Reference case, which generally represents current legislation and environmental regulations, including recent government actions for which implementing regulations were available as of October 31, 2013. The impacts on mercury emissions are expected to be negligible.

Mt, which is equivalent to the emissions resulting from the annual electricity use of 1.5 million homes.[12]

The value of the CO_2 reduction is calculated using a range of values per metric ton of CO_2 (otherwise known as the Social Cost of Carbon, or SCC) developed by a recent Federal interagency process.[13] The derivation of the SCC values is discussed in section IV.L. Using discount rates appropriate for each set of SCC values (see Table I.2), DOE estimates the present monetary value of the CO_2 emissions reduction is between $0.2 billion and $3.4 billion, with a value of $1.1 billion using the central SCC case represented by $40.5/t in 2015. Additionally, DOE estimates the present monetary value of the NO_X emissions reduction to be $0.06 billion to $0.15 billion at 7-percent and 3-percent discount rates, respectively.[14]

Table I.2 summarizes the national economic benefits and costs expected to result from the proposed standard for hearth products.

---

[12] Environmental Protection Agency. EPA GHG calculator (Last Accessed; December 23, 2014) (Available at: http://www.epa.gov/cleanenergy/energy-resources/calculator.html#results)

[13] Technical Update of the Social Cost of Carbon for Regulatory Impact Analysis Under Executive Order 12866, Interagency Working Group on Social Cost of Carbon, United States Government (May 2013; revised November 2013) (Available at: http://www.whitehouse.gov/sites/default/files/omb/assets/inforeg/technical-update-social-cost-of-carbon-for-regulator-impact-analysis.pdf).

[14] DOE is investigating valuation of avoided Hg and SO_2 emissions.

Table I.2 Summary of National Economic Benefits and Costs of Proposed Energy Conservation Standard for Hearth Products (TSL 1)*

Category	Present Value Billion 2013$	Discount Rate %
Benefits		
Consumer Operating Cost Savings	1.536	7
	4.128	3
CO_2 Reduction Monetized Value ($12.0/t case)**	0.226	5
CO_2 Reduction Monetized Value ($40.5/t case)**	1.098	3
CO_2 Reduction Monetized Value ($62.4/t case)**	1.763	2.5
CO_2 Reduction Monetized Value ($119/t case)**	3.405	3 (95th percentile)
NO_X Reduction Monetized Value (at $2,684/ton)**	0.058	7
	0.148	3
Total Benefits†	2.693	7
	5.373	3
Costs		
Consumer Incremental Installed Costs	0.505	7
	1.004	3
Total Net Benefits		
Including Emissions Reduction Monetized Value†	2.187	7
	4.369	3

* This table presents the costs and benefits associated with hearth products shipped in 2021-2050. These results include benefits to consumers that accrue after 2050 from the products purchased in 2021-2050. The results account for the incremental variable and fixed costs incurred by manufacturers due to the standard, some of which may be incurred in preparation for the rule.

** The CO_2 values represent global monetized values of the SCC, in 2013$, in 2015 under several scenarios of the updated SCC values. The first three cases use the averages of SCC distributions calculated using 5%, 3%, and 2.5% discount rates, respectively. The fourth case represents the 95th percentile of the SCC distribution calculated using a 3% discount rate. The SCC time series used by DOE incorporate an escalation factor. The value for NOx is the average of high and low values found in the literature.

† Total Benefits for both the 3% and 7% cases are derived using the series corresponding to average SCC with a 3-percent discount rate ($40.5/t in 2015).

The benefits and costs of today's proposed energy conservation standard, for hearth products sold in 2021-2050, can also be expressed in terms of annualized values. The annualized monetary values are the sum of: (1) the annualized national economic value of the benefits from consumer operation of products that meet the proposed new or amended standards (consisting primarily of operating cost savings from using less energy, minus increases in product purchase and installation costs, which is another way of representing consumer NPV), and (2) the annualized monetary value of the benefits of emission reductions, including CO_2 emission reductions.[15]

Although combining the values of operating savings and CO_2 emission reductions provides a useful perspective, two issues should be considered. First, the national operating savings are domestic U.S. consumer monetary savings that occur as a result of market transactions, whereas the value of CO_2 reductions is based on a global value. Second, the assessments of operating cost savings and CO_2 savings are performed with different methods that use different time frames for analysis. The national operating cost savings is measured for the lifetime of hearth products shipped in 2021-2050. The SCC values, on the other hand, reflect the present value of some future climate-related impacts resulting from the emission of one ton of carbon dioxide in each year. These impacts continue well beyond 2100.

Estimates of annualized benefits and costs of the proposed standard are shown in Table I.3. The results under the primary estimate are as follows. Using a 7-percent discount rate for benefits and costs other than CO_2 reduction (for which DOE used a 3-

---

[15] To convert the time-series of costs and benefits into annualized values, DOE calculated a present value in 2014, the year used for discounting the NPV of total consumer costs and savings. For the benefits, DOE calculated a present value associated with each year's shipments in the year in which the shipments occur (2020, 2030, etc.), and then discounted the present value from each year to 2014. The calculation uses discount rates of 3 and 7 percent for all costs and benefits except for the value of CO_2 reductions, for which DOE used case-specific discount rates. Using the present value, DOE then calculated the fixed annual payment over a 30-year period, starting in the compliance year that yields the same present value.

percent discount rate along with the average SCC series that uses a 3-percent discount rate ($40.5/t in 2015)), the cost of the hearth products standards proposed in this rule is $61.1 million per year in increased equipment costs, while the estimated benefits are $186 million per year in reduced equipment operating costs, $67 million per year in CO_2 reductions, and $7.0 million per year in reduced NO_X emissions. In this case, the net benefit would amount to $199 million per year. Using a 3-percent discount rate for all benefits and costs and the average SCC series that uses a 3-percent discount rate ($40.5/t in 2015), the estimated cost of the hearth products standards proposed in this rule is $61.2 million per year in increased equipment costs, while the estimated benefits are $251 million per year in reduced equipment operating costs, $67 million per year in CO_2 reductions, and $9.0 million per year in reduced NO_X emissions. In this case, the net benefit would amount to $266 million per year.

Table I.3 Annualized Benefits and Costs of Proposed Energy Conservation Standards for Hearth Products (TSL 1)

	Discount Rate %	Primary Estimate*	Low Net Benefits Estimate*	High Net Benefits Estimate*
		million 2013$/year		
Benefits				
Consumer Operating Cost Savings	7%	186	175	195
	3%	251	235	265
CO_2 Reduction Monetized Value ($12.0/t case)**	5%	20	20	20
CO_2 Reduction Monetized Value ($40.5/t case)**	3%	67	67	67
CO_2 Reduction Monetized Value ($62.4/t case)**	2.50%	98	98	98
CO_2 Reduction Monetized Value ($119/t case)**	3%	207	207	207
NOX Reduction Monetized Value (at $2,684/ton)**	7%	7.00	7.00	7.00
	3%	8.99	8.99	8.99
Total Benefits†	7% plus CO2 range	212 to 400	202 to 389	222 to 410
	7%	260	249	269
	3% plus CO2 range	280 to 468	264 to 452	294 to 482
	3%	327	311	341
Costs				
Consumer Incremental Equipment Costs	7%	61.1	61.1	61.1
	3%	61.2	61.2	61.2
Net Benefits				
Total†	7% plus CO2 range	151 to 339	141 to 328	161 to 349
	7%	199	188	208
	3% plus CO2 range	219 to 407	203 to 390	233 to 420
	3%	266	250	280

* This table presents the annualized costs and benefits associated with hearth products shipped in 2021-2050. These results include benefits to consumers that accrue after 2050 from the products purchased in 2021-2050. The results account for the incremental variable and fixed costs incurred by manufacturers due to the standard, some of which may be incurred in preparation for the rule. The Primary, Low Net Impacts, and High Net Impacts Estimates utilize projections of energy prices from the AEO 2014 Reference case, Low Estimate, and High Estimate, respectively. Incremental product costs are the same for each Estimate.

** The CO_2 values represent global monetized values of the SCC, in 2013\$, in 2015 under several scenarios of the updated SCC values. The first three cases use the averages of SCC distributions calculated using 5%, 3%, and 2.5% discount rates, respectively. The fourth case represents the 95th percentile of the SCC distribution calculated using a 3% discount rate. The SCC time series used by DOE incorporate an escalation factor. The value for NOx is the average of high and low values found in the literature.
† Total Benefits for both the 3% and 7% cases are derived using the series corresponding to the average SCC with a 3-percent discount rate (\$40.5/t in 2015). In the rows labeled "7% plus CO_2 range" and "3% plus CO_2 range," the operating cost and NO_X benefits are calculated using the labeled discount rate, and those values are added to the full range of CO_2 values.

D. Conclusion

DOE has tentatively concluded that the proposed standard represents the maximum improvement in energy efficiency that is technologically feasible and economically justified, and would result in significant conservation of energy. DOE further notes that products achieving the proposed standard are already commercially available. Based on the analyses described previously, DOE has tentatively concluded that the benefits of the proposed standards to the Nation (energy savings, positive NPV of consumer benefits, consumer LCC savings, and emission reductions) would outweigh the burdens (loss of INPV for manufacturers and LCC increases for some consumers).

Based on consideration of the public comments DOE receives in response to this notice and related information collected and analyzed during the course of this rulemaking, DOE may adopt the standard proposed in this notice, or some combination of options that incorporate the proposed standard in part.

II. Introduction

The following section briefly discusses the statutory authority underlying today's proposal, as well as some of the relevant historical background related to the establishment of standards for hearth products.

A. Authority

Title III, Part B of the Energy Policy and Conservation Act of 1975 (EPCA or the Act), Pub. L. 94-163 (42 U.S.C. 6291-6309, as codified) established the Energy Conservation Program for Consumer Products Other Than Automobiles, a program designed to improve energy efficiency for consumer products and certain commercial and industrial equipment. In addition to specifying a list of covered residential products and commercial equipment, EPCA, as amended, contains provisions that enable the Secretary of Energy to classify additional types of consumer products as covered products. (42 U.S.C. 6292(a)(20)) Specifically, for a given product to be classified as a covered product, the Secretary must determine that:

(A)   Classifying the product as a covered product is necessary or appropriate for the purposes of carrying out EPCA; and

(B)   The average annual per-household energy use by products of such type is likely to exceed 100 kilowatt-hours (or its Btu equivalent) per year.

(42 U.S.C. 6292(b)(1)(A) and (B))

For the Secretary to prescribe an energy conservation standard pursuant to 42 U.S.C. 6295(o) and (p) for covered products added pursuant to 42 U.S.C. 6292(a)(20) and (b)(1), the Secretary must also determine that:

(A)　The average household energy use of the type (or class) of products has exceeded 150 kWh (or its Btu equivalent) per household for any 12-month period;

(B)　The aggregate 12-month household energy use of the type (or class) of products has exceeded 4.2 TWh;

(C)　Substantial improvement in energy efficiency is technologically feasible; and

(D)　Application of a labeling rule under 42 U.S.C. 6294 is unlikely to be sufficient to induce manufacturers to produce, and consumers and other persons to purchase, covered products of such type (or class) that achieve the maximum energy efficiency that is technologically feasible and economically justified.

(42 U.S.C. 6295(l)(1)(A)-(D))[16]

---

[16] DOE notes that a drafting error arose at the time Congress adopted the amendments to EPCA contained in the Energy Independence and Security Act of 2007 (EISA 2007), Pub. L. 110-140. As part of the EISA 2007 amendments, Congress added metal halide lamp fixtures to the list of specifically enumerated covered products at 42 U.S.C. 6292(a)(19) and shifted the provision for the Secretary to classify "any other type" of a consumer product as a covered product to 42 U.S.C. 6292(a)(20). However, Congress did not similarly amend the criteria and other requirements for setting energy conservation standards for "other" covered products in 42 U.S.C. 6295(l)(1) and (2). The provisions in 42 U.S.C. 6295(l) continued to refer to standards for "any type" of covered product, while continuing to refer to 42 U.S.C. 6292(a)(20). Clearly, the provisions at 42 U.S.C. 6295(l) were intended to apply more broadly than to metal halide lamp fixtures,

Pursuant to EPCA, DOE's energy conservation program for covered products consists essentially of four parts: (1) testing; (2) labeling; (3) establishing Federal energy conservation standards; and (4) certification and enforcement procedures. The Federal Trade Commission (FTC) is primarily responsible for labeling, and DOE implements the remainder of the program.

DOE must follow specific statutory criteria for prescribing standards for covered products, including hearth products. As indicated previously, 42 U.S.C. 6295(o) and (p) contain specific criteria for establishing or amending energy conservation standards for covered products. Any new or amended standard for a covered product must be designed to achieve the maximum improvement in energy efficiency that is technologically feasible and economically justified. (42 U.S.C. 6295(o)(2)(A) and (3)(B)) Furthermore, DOE may not adopt any standard that would not result in the significant conservation of energy. (42 U.S.C. 6295(o)(3)) Moreover, DOE may not prescribe a standard: (1) for certain products, including hearth products, if no test procedure has been established for the product,[17] or (2) if DOE determines by rule that the proposed standard is not technologically feasible or economically justified. (42 U.S.C. 6295(o)(3)(A)-(B)) In deciding whether a proposed standard is economically justified, after receiving comments on the proposed standard, DOE must determine whether the benefits of the standard

---

so DOE continues to apply this provision as if the drafting error had not occurred. To do otherwise would render the provision at 42 U.S.C. 6295(l) a nullity, thereby thwarting DOE's ability to set energy conservation standards for newly covered products, an outcome which Congress could not have intended.
[17] As discussed in section III.D, DOE is not prescribing a test procedure because it is unnecessary for the prescriptive energy conservation standards that were considered for this NOPR.

exceed its burdens. (42 U.S.C. 6295(o)(2)(B)(i)) DOE must make this determination by, to the greatest extent practicable, considering the following seven factors:

(1) The economic impact of the standard on manufacturers and consumers of the products subject to the standard;

(2) The savings in operating costs throughout the estimated average life of the covered products in the type (or class) compared to any increase in the price, initial charges, or maintenance expenses for the covered products that are likely to result from the standard;

(3) The total projected amount of energy (or as applicable, water) savings likely to result directly from the standard;

(4) Any lessening of the utility or the performance of the covered products likely to result from the standard;

(5) The impact of any lessening of competition, as determined in writing by the Attorney General, that is likely to result from the standard;

(6) The need for national energy and water conservation; and

(7) Other factors the Secretary of Energy (Secretary) considers relevant. (42 U.S.C. 6295(o)(2)(B)(i)(I)–(VII))

EPCA, as codified, also contains what is known as an "anti-backsliding" provision, which prevents the Secretary from prescribing any amended standard that either increases the maximum allowable energy use or decreases the minimum required energy efficiency of a covered product. (42 U.S.C. 6295(o)(1)) Also, the Secretary may not prescribe an amended or new standard if interested persons have established by a preponderance of evidence that the standard is likely to result in the unavailability in the United States of any covered product type (or class) with performance characteristics (including reliability), features, sizes, capacities, and volumes that are substantially the same as those generally available in the United States. (42 U.S.C. 6295(o)(4))

Further, EPCA, as codified, establishes a rebuttable presumption that a standard is economically justified if the Secretary finds that the additional cost to the consumer of purchasing a product complying with an energy conservation standard level will be less than three times the value of the energy savings during the first year that the consumer will receive as a result of the standard, as calculated under the applicable test procedure. (42 U.S.C. 6295(o)(2)(B)(iii))

Additionally, 42 U.S.C. 6295(q)(1) specifies requirements when promulgating an energy conservation standard for a covered product that has two or more subcategories. DOE must specify a different standard level for a type or class of covered product that has the same function or intended use, if DOE determines that products within such group: (A) consume a different kind of energy from that consumed by other covered products within such type (or class); or (B) have a capacity or other performance-related feature that other products within such type (or class) do not have and such feature justifies a higher or lower standard. (42 U.S.C. 6295(q)(1)) In determining whether a performance-related feature justifies a different standard for a group of products, DOE must consider such factors as the utility to the consumer of the feature and other factors

DOE deems appropriate. Id. Any rule prescribing such a standard must include an explanation of the basis on which such higher or lower level was established. (42 U.S.C. 6295(q)(2))

Federal energy conservation requirements generally supersede State laws or regulations concerning energy conservation testing, labeling, and standards. (42 U.S.C. 6297(a)–(c)) DOE may, however, grant waivers of Federal preemption for particular State laws or regulations, in accordance with the procedures and other provisions set forth under 42 U.S.C. 6297(d).

In addition, pursuant to other amendments contained in EISA 2007, any final rule for new or amended energy conservation standards promulgated after July 1, 2010 is required to address standby mode and off mode energy use. (42 U.S.C. 6295(gg)(3)) Specifically, when DOE adopts a standard for a covered product after that date, it must, if justified by the criteria for adoption of standards under EPCA (42 U.S.C. 6295(o)), incorporate standby mode and off mode energy use into a single standard, or, if that is not feasible, adopt a separate standard for such energy use for that product. (42 U.S.C. 6295(gg)(3)(A)-(B))

Finally, it is noted that under 42 U.S.C. 6295(m), the agency must periodically review established energy conservation standards for a covered product. Under this requirement, such review must be conducted no later than 6 years from the issuance of any final rule establishing or amending a standard for a covered product.

B. Background

DOE has not previously conducted an energy conservation standards rulemaking for hearth products. Consequently, there are currently no Federal energy conservation standards for hearth products.

On December 31, 2013, DOE published a notice of proposed determination (NOPD) of coverage to classify hearth products as covered products under EPCA. 78 FR 79638. In the proposed determination of coverage, DOE presented its preliminary findings relating to the energy use of hearth products to determine whether they could be classified as a type of covered product under the requirements of 42 U.S.C. 6292(b)(1)(A) and (B), and whether they would meet the criteria for DOE to prescribe an energy conservation standard under 42 U.S.C. 6295(l)(1)(A)-(D). (See section II.A for a discussion of these statutory criteria.) DOE also proposed to define a "hearth product" as "a gas-fired appliance that simulates a solid-fueled fireplace or presents a flame pattern (for aesthetics or other purpose) and that may provide space heating directly to the space in which it is installed." 78 FR 79638, 79640 (Dec. 31, 2013). The proposed determination is still pending, but as discussed in section IV.A, DOE is using the proposed definition to delineate the scope of this NOPR. In addition, DOE has considered some of the comments submitted in response to the proposed coverage determination, which are relevant to the development of proposed energy conservation standards for hearth products and addresses those comments as applicable in this NOPR.

III. General Discussion

A. Scope of Coverage

In the December 2013 NOPD, DOE proposed to adopt a definition of hearth product that means a gas-fired appliance that simulates a solid-fueled fireplace or presents a flame pattern (for aesthetics or other purpose) and that may provide space heating directly to the space in which it is installed.

Based upon the scope arising from this proposed definition and after making the necessary energy use calculations, DOE tentatively determined that hearth products would meet the relevant statutory criteria so as to justify coverage as a consumer product under EPCA, and provided the relevant justifications in the notice. 78 FR 79638, 79640-41 (Dec. 31, 2013). In the December 2013 NOPD, DOE provided examples of several common hearth product types that would be covered under the proposed definition, including vented decorative hearth products, vented heater hearth products, vented gas logs, gas stoves, outdoor hearth products, and vent-less hearth products. Id. at 79640.

DOE used the definition proposed in the December 2013 NOPD (as stated above) to determine the scope of this NOPR. .

In setting forth new energy conservation standards for any type of covered product, EPCA requires DOE to determine that: (1) the product consumes more than 150 kilowatt-hours (or its Btu equivalent) per household in any 12 month period occurring before such a determination; (2) the aggregate energy use within the United States was

26

more than 4,200,000,000 kilowatt-hours (kWh) (or its Btu equivalent) in any 12 month period occurring before such a determination; (3) substantial improvement in energy efficiency for the products is technologically feasible; and (4) the application of labeling is not likely to be sufficient for manufacturers to produce or for consumers to purchase products that would achieve the maximum energy efficiency which is technologically feasible and economically justified. (42 U.S.C. 6295(l)(1)(A)-(D))

With regards to the first and second criteria, DOE has estimated the average household consumption to be 7.5 million Btu (equal to 2,198 kWh), and aggregate national energy use to be 95 trillion Btu (equal to 27,800,000,000 kWh) for currently-installed hearth products. (Details on these calculations can be found in chapter 7 of the NOPR TSD.) With regard to the third criterion, DOE found that several technologies are available to substantially improve the energy efficiency (or reduce the overall energy consumption) of hearth products in standby-mode. These technologies are discussed in section IV.C.2. Finally, with regard to the last criterion, DOE found through product literature review and manufacturer interviews that labeling is already often included in manuals that suggest users extinguish the pilot light when the product is not in use. However, for products such as those that include a millivolt gas valve, the user must allow the standing pilot to remain on so that the valve can be activated or deactivated by a thermostat or remote control. Further, regardless of instructions in the manual, DOE understands that a significant percentage of consumers allow the standing pilot light to burn year-round. DOE has, therefore, tentatively determined that the application of labeling is not sufficient to result in the maximum energy savings that would be

27

technologically feasible and economically justified (i.e., the savings achievable through the proposal presented, in this NOPR). In summary, DOE has tentatively determined that hearth products, under the proposed definition, meet all the criteria for establishing energy conservation standards under EPCA.

The purpose of this NOPR is to propose energy conservation standards for products that, together with the December 2013 proposed coverage determination, would establish coverage and energy conservation standards for hearth products. DOE has not previously conducted an energy conservation standards rulemaking for hearth products. If, after public comment, DOE issues a final determination of coverage for this type of product, DOE would consider adoption of the energy conservation standards for hearth products proposed in this NOPR.

DOE received several comments in response to the December 2013 NOPD that pertained to the definition and broad range of hearth product types. DOE notes that in general, these comments pertain to the determination of coverage process, not the energy conservation standards process, and so DOE will respond in full to these comments as part of the determination of coverage process. However, DOE acknowledges that certain comments on the December 2013 NOPD do have relevance for this NOPR and addresses them below and in section III.C in relevant part.

Multiple commenters in response to the December 2013 NOPD stated that the proposed definition for "hearth product" is too broad, and that a reasonable energy conservation standard regulation could not be achieved for a definition that encompassed such a wide variety of products. (Hearth, Patio and Barbecue Association (HPBA), No. 5 at p. 6; National Propane Gas Association (NPGA), No. 7 at p. 2; RH Peterson, No. 8 at p. 2; Rasmussen, No. 9 at p. 2; Hearth & Home Technologies (HHT), No. 11 at p. 1; Empire, No. 12 at p. 1; Air-Conditioning, Heating, and Refrigeration Institute (AHRI), No. 15 at p. 2; Wolf Steel, No. 4 at p. 2; American Public Gas Association (APGA), No. 14 at p. 2) In response, DOE acknowledges that the hearth products market is broad and encompasses a wide range of products. DOE recognizes this as one product market and has proposed a definition accordingly. Nevertheless, DOE has chosen to conduct its analyses for this rulemaking using hearth product groups that have similar characteristics. For details about the physical characteristics of each product group for analysis, see chapter 5 of the NOPR TSD.

DOE seeks additional comment regarding its proposed definition for hearth products found in the December 2013 NOPD and this is identified as Issue 1 in section VII.E "Issues on Which DOE Seeks Comment."

B. Prescriptive Requirement for Standby Mode

As discussed previously, this NOPR proposes to adopt a prescriptive design requirement that would reduce hearth product energy consumption in standby mode. This design requirement would not affect energy consumption or efficiency in active mode. EPCA defines "active mode" energy consumption as the condition in which an appliance is connected to a main power source, has been activated, and provides one or more main functions. (42 U.S.C. 6295(gg)(1)(A)(i)) DOE notes that when the main burner of a hearth product is off, the product can no longer be considered in active mode. EPCA defines "off mode" as the condition in which the product is connected to its main power source and is not providing any standby or active mode function. (42 U.S.C. 6295(gg)(1)(A)(ii)) DOE has tentatively concluded that this occurs for hearth products when the main burner is not lit and, for models with continuously-burning pilots, when the pilot light is not lit.

EPCA defines "standby mode" energy consumption as the condition in which an appliance is connected to a main power source (in this case natural gas or propane connection) and facilitates the activation of other modes (including active mode) by remote switch, internal sensor, or timer, or serves other continuous functions. (42 U.S.C. 6295(gg)(1)(A)(iii)) DOE notes that the standing pilot may serve several continuous functions. The continuous pilot may provide a safety function by proving gas is lit before opening the valve for the main burner. In the case of an unvented hearth product, the standing pilot provides a means for ensuring that oxygen levels in the room remain at a safe level through incorporation of an oxygen depletion sensor. In the case of a millivolt gas valve, a standing pilot facilitates activation of active mode using a remote control; this is accomplished by the pilot light heating a thermopile, which produces a voltage difference, thereby allowing use with electronic controls. Therefore, DOE has concluded that the standing pilot qualifies as standby mode energy use.

DOE estimated the average annual amount of energy consumed by the main burner and by the standing pilot for each hearth product group.[18,19] These estimates can be found in Table III.1. Active mode operation may use fossil fuels more intensively, but standby mode uses fossil fuels over significantly more hours on an annual basis.

Table III.1 Average Annual Energy Use in Active Mode (Main Burner) and Standby Mode (Standing Pilot)

Hearth Product Analysis Group	Main Burner Energy Consumption (MMBtu/yr)	Standing Pilot Energy Consumption (MMBtu/yr)
Vented Fireplaces, Inserts, and Stoves	5.19	3.99
Unvented Fireplaces, Inserts, and Stoves	4.47	3.52
Vented Gas Log Sets	8.31	3.13
Unvented Gas Log Set	4.53	2.29
Outdoor	7.02	3.52
Weighted Average	**5.28**	**3.54**

As shown in Table III.1, the standing pilot energy consumption makes up a significant portion of the overall energy consumption for hearth products. Further, the energy savings that can be achieved through disallowing standing pilot lights is greater than the savings that could be achieved through increasing the active mode efficiency via a performance standard. An active mode performance standard would only partially reduce the active mode energy consumption, whereas a prescriptive requirement to remove the standing pilot could be applied to all hearth product types and would reduce the standing pilot energy consumption to zero.

---

[18] Description of the hearth product groups can be found in chapter 5 of the NOPR TSD.

[19] These values are calculated as the main burner operating hours multiplied by the average input capacity and the standing pilot operating hours multiplied by the average pilot light input rate, respectively. The operating hours can be found in chapter 7 of the NOPR TSD.

DOE also considered whether a maximum energy use performance standard would be appropriate for hearth products in active mode. DOE recognizes that hearth products are available for a wide range of input capacities depending on the consumer's needs. In general, the gas input is proportional to the size of the hearth product. A performance standard for hearth products that establishes a maximum energy use would likely eliminate certain sizes of hearth products from the market and could negatively impact the utility of the product.

DOE considered several individual technologies that could potentially reduce the energy consumption of hearth products as discussed in section IV.A.3. All of the technology options identified, except for the electronic ignition, pertain to active mode energy use. Based on manufacturer feedback, DOE tentatively concluded that five of the technologies considered (air-to-fuel ratio, burner port design, simulated log design, burner pan media or bead type, and reflective combustion zone surfaces) would result in immeasurable or negligible active mode energy savings. Two of the considered technologies – the circulating fan and the condensing heat exchanger – would only apply to a subset of hearth products. Also, these two technology options may only be implemented in those types of units that incorporate an enclosure to house the components (i.e., they would not be applicable for gas log sets and certain types of outdoor hearths).

DOE has tentatively determined that all standby fossil fuel consumption would be eliminated by disallowing the use of standing pilots.[20] When turning on a gas hearth appliance, a pilot light is first ignited before gas flows to the main burner and is lighted. The pilot light generally may be constant-burning ("standing") or intermittent. In the case of a standing pilot, the pilot light continues to consume gas even when the main burner is not consuming gas, unless the consumer chooses to shut off gas to the pilot as well.

The standby mode operation and energy use of hearth products are functions of ignition type. Ignition types for all hearth products fall under three categories: (1) match-lit; (2), constant-burning or "standing" pilot; and (3) electronic ignition. For match-lit ignition systems, in order to ignite the burner, the user must manually turn on the gas flow and light the main burner with a match, lighter, or other device. After use, the user should manually turn off the gas valve, thereby reducing the fuel flow to zero when the product is not in operation. Therefore, match-lit products do not consume energy when not in active mode. For products with electronic ignitions, the most common approach is an intermittent pilot ignition. In this system, upon a call for the burner to ignite (either from the user or a thermostat), a spark lights a pilot, which in turn ignites the main burner. When the main burner shuts off, the pilot also shuts off, and, thus, any energy use in standby mode is electrical. DOE has tentatively determined this electrical consumption is *de minimis*.[20] For constant-burning pilots, the user must manually light the pilot each time it is extinguished, either manually with a match or through the use of a piezo-igniter. Then the pilot in turn lights the main burner. However, in this case, the

---

[20] See section III.I for discussion of electrical standby consumption for hearth products.

33

pilot remains on after the main burner shuts off, awaiting future calls to ignite the burner. Therefore, hearth products with standing pilots continue to use gas typically at a rate between 700 and 1,200 Btu/h when the pilot light is not extinguished. Since match-lit hearth products consume no energy in standby mode and off mode and since the electrical consumption of electronic ignitions has been tentatively determined to be *de minimis,* disallowing the use of constant-burning pilot ignition systems would effectively eliminate all standby mode energy use for these products. These characteristics are common to the standby mode operation across all hearth products.

Therefore, while an energy efficiency performance standard for active mode and the technology options to achieve efficiency improvements could result in only a fractional reduction of energy consumption for a subset of hearth products, disallowing the standing pilot ignition type would eliminate all standby fossil fuel use for hearth products. Of the three general ignition types for hearth products – match-lit, standing pilot, and electronic ignition – only the standing pilot ignition systems contribute substantially to standby mode energy, so disallowing their use would effectively eliminate standby mode energy consumption of hearth products.

DOE also considered performance standards for standby mode. Since the standing pilot light is used for several functions, reducing the allowable use during standby mode would hinder these products from providing these functions. (Note: electronic ignitions are capable of providing the same functions as standing pilot ignition systems, and so disallowing standing pilots will not eliminate this utility from the market.) DOE is also unaware, as stated in section IV.A.3, of technologies for substantially reducing the consumption of pilot lights. Additionally, DOE has determined that a design requirement would be more effective and easier to implement than a performance standard addressing standby mode. A performance standard would likely also require a test procedure to be established and would increase manufacturer burden due to testing requirements.

In summary, DOE has tentatively concluded the following:

(1) A potential maximum energy use performance standard for active mode would likely restrict the sizes of available hearth products, eliminating part of the market.

(2) The technology options available for reducing the active mode energy consumption of hearth products either result in immeasurable or negligible energy savings, or only apply to a subset of hearth products resulting in limited opportunity for energy savings;

(3) A prescriptive requirement that disallows the use of standing pilot ignition systems would eliminate all standby mode fossil fuel use,[20] which represents a large fraction of the overall energy use for hearth products;

(4) An performance standard for standby mode would be less effective than a prescriptive requirement disallowing standing pilot ignitions, and would result in more manufacturer burden due to testing requirements; and

(5) There are no technology options available to substantially reduce the energy consumption of pilot lights other than removing them; and

(6) There is no associated public health or safety issue associated with replacing any constant-burning pilot with an intermittent pilot ignition system for the hearth products identified in this proposal. (DOE also requests comment on this assumption and this is identified as Issue 2 in section VII.E "Issues on Which DOE Seeks Comment.")

For the reasons cited above, DOE has focused the analysis for this NOPR on a prescriptive requirement for standby mode energy use that would disallow the use of a constant-burning pilot light. DOE recognizes that an equivalent performance standard and test procedure could be proposed such that would measure the standby mode gas consumption and ensure it is zero. However, such a standard and accompanying test procedure would be unduly burdensome, since confirming that a hearth product does not have the components necessary for a standing pilot light ensures that there is no standby mode gas consumption.

C. Product Classes

In evaluating and establishing energy conservation standards, DOE generally divides covered products into classes by the type of energy used or by capacity or other performance-related feature that justifies a different standard for products having such feature. (See 42 U.S.C. 6295(q)) In deciding whether a feature justifies a different standard, DOE must consider factors such as the utility of the feature to users. Id. DOE may also consider other factors it deems appropriate when determining product classes. Id. DOE normally establishes different energy conservation standards for different product classes based on these criteria.

According to the proposed definition of "hearth product" in the December 2013

NOPD, a hearth product is a gas-fired appliance that simulates a solid-fueled fireplace or

presents a flame pattern. 78 FR 79638, 79640 (Dec. 31, 2013). In the proposed

definition, DOE acknowledges that hearth products may serve one or more functions to

the consumer, stating that a hearth product under the proposed definition "presents a

flame pattern (for aesthetics or other purpose)" and "*may* provide space heating." Id.

DOE also suggested several examples of product types that would be covered under such

a definition, including vented decorative hearth products, vented heater hearth products,

vented gas logs, gas stoves, outdoor hearth products, and vent-less hearth products.

DOE also received several comments that suggested an efficiency metric is

unachievable or disadvantageous for decorative products or gas log sets. (HPBA, No. 5

at p. 9; American Gas Association (AGA), No. 6 at p. 2; RH Peterson, No. 8 at p. 3;

Rasmussen, No. 9 at p. 2; Wolf Steel, No. 4 at p. 1; AHRI, No. 15 at p. 3-4) Wolf Steel

also suggested labeling requirements that would clearly identify decorative and heater

products. (Wolf Steel, No.4 at p.4)

In addition to the December 2013 NOPD comments, DOE also examined current

product offerings and product literature, performed teardown analyses (described in

section IV.C.3.a), and conducted manufacturer interviews in an effort to better

understand the market and feature sets unique to various hearth products to determine

whether capacity or performance-related features would justify different standards.

Based on this analysis, DOE has tentatively concluded the following and seeks comment (Issue 3 in section VII.E) regarding these conclusions:

(1) Within the hearth industry, there is no universally accepted definition or set of defining features or other physical characteristics for what constitutes different categories of hearth products. The distinction between products is sometimes, though not always, defined by whether the product is vented or unvented. However, even within these groupings, the same product is sometimes certified to multiple ANSI standards and in other cases apparently are certified to different ANSI standards. For example, unvented gas log sets are sometimes certified to the ANSI Z21.60 decorative gas-fired appliance standard[21] in addition to the ANSI Z21.11.2 unvented heater standard.[22] Vented products are often advertised with an AFUE or thermal efficiency rating, and may be certified to either or both the ANSI Z21.88 vented heater fireplace standard[23] or the ANSI Z21.50 vented fireplace standard.[24]

(2) Hearth products encompass a wide range of configurations to serve size, space, and other constraints. Fireplaces, freestanding stoves, and gas log sets vary widely

---

[21] Latest version is ANSI Z21.60-2012, *Decorative gas appliances for installation in solid-fuel burning fireplaces* (Available at: http://shop.csa.ca/en/canada/gas-fired-domestic-and-commercial-heating-equipment-and-air-conditioning/ansi-z2160-2012csa-226-2012/invt/27019512012).

[22] Latest version is ANSI Z21.11.2-2013, *Gas-fired room heaters, volume II, unvented room heaters* (Available at: http://shop.csa.ca/en/canada/gas-fired-domestic-and-commercial-heating-equipment-and-air-conditioning/ansi-z21112-2013/invt/27017312013).

[23] Latest version is ANSI Z21.88-2014, *Vented gas fireplace heaters* (Available at: http://shop.csa.ca/en/canada/gas-fired-domestic-and-commercial-heating-equipment-and-air-conditioning/ansi-z2188-2014csa-233-2014/invt/27016252014).

[24] Latest version is ANSI Z21.50-2014, *Vented gas fireplaces* (Available at: http://shop.csa.ca/en/canada/gas-fired-domestic-and-commercial-heating-equipment-and-air-conditioning/ansi-z2150-2014csa-222-2014-/invt/27020142014).

in their physical characteristics, as well as input capacities.

(3) Gas log sets are installed in existing fireboxes and masonry fireplaces. Therefore, the manufacturer of a gas log set has virtually no control over an array of factors that would affect the efficiency of their product, including the firebox size, shape, material, and in the case of vented gas logs, the amount of draft.

DOE acknowledges that these issues represent challenges in establishing product classes (because differentiating between different types is often difficult due to the similarities of different types of hearths) or in developing an efficiency metric that would apply for all hearth products.

In comments in response to the December 2013 NOPD, HPBA stated "under EPCA, a 'covered product' is a type of product defined by a common functional utility and for which a common efficiency descriptor can be applied." HPBA further stated: "the premise that a 'covered product' must be defined by a common functional utility is the only premise that makes sense in EPCA's context, because the 'efficiency' of a product can be determined only by reference to its function." (HPBA, No. 5 at p. 7)

While DOE considered product classes in light of the issues presented above, these considerations pertain to the active mode operation of hearth products. As discussed in section III.B, DOE has tentatively concluded that a prescriptive requirement for standby mode (i.e., requiring the removal of standing pilot ignition systems) would have the most energy savings potential and would apply across all types of hearth products. Thus, DOE's analysis focused on standby mode. DOE found considerable similarity across hearth products in their standby mode functionality, components, and energy use.

In summary, when DOE analyzed the hearth market to consider whether to establish product classes based on standby mode energy consumption, it found that there is a substantial similarity among hearth products of all types, in that the primary mechanism of energy consumption in standby mode is a constant-burning pilot. Therefore, DOE has tentatively concluded that the establishment of product classes is not necessary for the energy conservation standards proposed by this NOPR.

D. Test Procedure

In this NOPR, DOE is proposing to adopt a prescriptive design requirement for hearth products. Specifically, DOE is proposing to disallow the use of a continuously-burning pilot light in these products. DOE typically establishes test procedures by which products must be tested in order to certify compliance with an energy conservation standard. Because this proposed standard is a design requirement and not a performance standard (*i.e.*, minimum efficiency or maximum energy consumption), DOE has tentatively concluded that a test procedure is not required in order to determine compliance with the standard.

EPCA states, in relevant part, that an amended or new standard may not be adopted if a test procedure has not been established for the relevant product type or class. (42 U.S.C. 6295(o)(3)(A)) However, later sections of EPCA acknowledge that DOE may establish prescriptive design requirements that by nature would not require a test procedure. For determining compliance with standards, EPCA requires use of the test procedures and criteria prescribed in 42 U.S.C. 6293, except for design standards. (42 U.S.C. 6295(s)) EPCA also states that a test procedure need not be prescribed if one cannot be designed to reasonably measure energy efficiency, energy use, water use, or annual operating cost, and not be unduly burdensome to conduct. (42 U.S.C. 6293(d)(1)) EPCA requires that a determination be published in the Federal Register providing justification for such case. Id.

DOE contends that any test procedure to determine whether a hearth product has a continuously-burning pilot would be unduly burdensome to conduct in light of fact that the proposed standard is in the form of a prescriptive design requirement. While a test could be conducted to measure standby mode fuel consumption (which would indicate the presence of a continuously-burning pilot if such consumption is greater than zero), such a test procedure is not required since removing standing pilots will effectively reduce standby mode gas consumption to zero. Further, determining whether a continuously-burning pilot is present on the unit can be easily assessed without testing through a review of operating instructions and physical inspection. Therefore, DOE has tentatively concluded that adoption of a test procedure is not required for establishing the proposed energy conservation standards for hearth products since that standard is based

41

upon a design requirement. If DOE were to consider a performance standard for hearth products in the future, the agency would develop an appropriate test procedure at that time.

E. Technological Feasibility

1. General

In each energy conservation standards rulemaking, DOE conducts a screening analysis based on information gathered on all current technology and prototype designs that could improve the efficiency of the products or equipment that are the subject of the rulemaking. As the first step in such an analysis, DOE develops a list of technology options for consideration in consultation with manufacturers, design engineers, and other interested parties. DOE then determines which of those means for improving efficiency or reducing energy use are technologically feasible. DOE considers technologies incorporated in commercially-available products or in working prototypes to be technologically feasible. 10 CFR part 430, subpart C, appendix A, section 4(a)(4)(i).

After DOE has determined that particular technology options are technologically feasible, it further evaluates each technology option in light of the following additional screening criteria: (1) practicability to manufacture, install, and service; (2) adverse impacts on product utility or availability; and (3) adverse impacts on health or safety. 10 CFR part 430, subpart C, appendix A, section 4(a)(4)(ii)-(iv). Additionally, it is DOE policy not to include in its analysis any proprietary technology that is a unique pathway to achieving a certain efficiency level. Section IV.B of this notice discusses the results of the screening analysis for hearth products, particularly the designs DOE considered, those it screened out, and those that are the basis for the trial standard levels (TSLs) in this rulemaking. For further details on the screening analysis for this rulemaking, see chapter 4 of the NOPR technical support document (TSD).

2. Maximum Technologically Feasible Levels

When DOE proposes to adopt an amended standard for a type or class of covered product, it must determine the maximum improvement in energy efficiency or maximum reduction in energy use that is technologically feasible for such product. (42 U.S.C. 6295(p)(1)) Accordingly, in the engineering analysis, DOE determined the maximum technologically feasible (max-tech) improvements in energy use for hearth products, using the design parameters for the least energy-intensive products available on the market or in working prototypes. The max-tech level that DOE determined for this rulemaking are described in section IV.C of this proposed rule and in chapter 5 of the NOPR TSD.

F. Energy Savings

1. Determination of Savings

For each TSL, DOE projected energy savings from the products that are the subject of this rulemaking purchased in the 30-year period that begins in the year of compliance with standards (2021–2050).[25] The savings are measured over the entire

---

[25] DOE also presents a sensitivity analysis that considers impacts for products shipped in a 9-year period.

lifetime of products purchased in the 30-year analysis period.[26] DOE quantified the energy savings attributable to each TSL as the difference in energy consumption between the new standards case and the base case. The base case represents a projection of energy consumption in the absence of energy conservation standards, and it considers market forces and policies that affect demand for more-efficient products.

DOE used its national impact analysis (NIA) spreadsheet model to estimate energy savings from potential standards for the products that are the subject of this rulemaking. The NIA spreadsheet model (described in section IV.H of this notice) calculates energy savings in site energy, which is the energy directly consumed by products at the locations where they are used. For electricity, DOE reports national energy savings on an annual basis in terms of primary (source) energy savings, which is the savings in the energy that is used to generate and transmit the site electricity. To calculate the primary energy savings, DOE derives annual conversion factors from the model used to prepare the Energy Information Administration's (EIA) most recent Annual Energy Outlook (AEO).

DOE also estimates full-fuel-cycle (FFC) energy savings, as discussed in DOE's statement of policy and notice of policy amendment. 76 FR 51282 (August 18, 2011), as amended at 77 FR 49701 (August 17, 2012). The FFC metric includes the energy

---

[26] In the past, DOE presented energy savings results for only the 30-year period that begins in the year of compliance. In the calculation of economic impacts, however, DOE considered operating cost savings measured over the entire lifetime of products purchased in the 30-year period. DOE has chosen to modify its presentation of national energy savings to be consistent with the approach used for its national economic analysis.

consumed in extracting, processing, and transporting primary fuels (*i.e.*, coal, natural gas, petroleum fuels), and, thus, presents a more complete picture of the impacts of energy conservation standards. DOE's approach is based on the calculation of an FFC multiplier for each of the energy types used by covered products or equipment. For more information on FFC energy savings, see section IV.H.1.

2. Significance of Savings

To adopt energy conservation standards for a covered product, DOE must determine that such action would result in "significant" energy savings. (42 U.S.C. 6295(o)(3)(B)) Although the term "significant" is not defined in the Act, the U.S. Court of Appeals for the District of Columbia Circuit, in Natural Resources Defense Council v. Herrington, 768 F.2d 1355, 1373 (D.C. Cir. 1985), opined that Congress intended "significant" energy savings in the context of EPCA to be savings that were not "genuinely trivial." The energy savings for all of the trial standard levels considered in this rulemaking, including the proposed standards (presented in section V.C), are nontrivial, and, therefore, DOE considers them "significant" within the meaning of section 325 of EPCA.

G. Economic Justification

1. Specific Criteria

EPCA provides seven factors to be evaluated in determining whether a potential energy conservation standard is economically justified. (42 U.S.C. 6295(o)(2)(B)(i)(I)-

(VII)) The following sections discuss how DOE has addressed each of those seven factors in this rulemaking.

a. Economic Impact on Manufacturers and Consumers

In determining the impacts of a potential energy conservation standard on manufacturers, DOE conducts a manufacturer impact analysis (MIA), as discussed in section IV.J. DOE first uses an annual cash-flow approach to determine the quantitative impacts. This step includes both a short-term assessment—based on the cost and capital requirements during the period between when a regulation is issued and when entities must comply with the regulation—and a long-term assessment over a 30-year period. The industry-wide impacts analyzed include: (1) INPV, which values the industry on the basis of expected future cash flows; (2) cash flows by year; (3) changes in revenue and income; and (4) other measures of impact, as appropriate. Second, DOE analyzes and reports the impacts on different types of manufacturers, including impacts on small manufacturers. Third, DOE considers the impact of standards on domestic manufacturer employment and manufacturing capacity, as well as the potential for standards to result in plant closures and loss of capital investment. Finally, DOE takes into account cumulative impacts of various DOE regulations and other regulatory requirements on manufacturers.

For individual consumers, measures of economic impact include the changes in LCC and PBP associated with new or amended standards. These measures are discussed further in the following section. For consumers in the aggregate, DOE also calculates the national net present value of the economic impacts applicable to a particular rulemaking.

DOE also evaluates the LCC impacts of potential standards on identifiable subgroups of consumers that may be affected disproportionately by a national standard.

b. Savings in Operating Costs Compared to Increase in Price (LCC and PBP)

EPCA requires DOE to consider the savings in operating costs throughout the estimated average life of the covered product in the type (or class) compared to any increase in the price of, or in the initial charges for, or maintenance expenses of, the covered product that are likely to result from a standard. (42 U.S.C. 6295(o)(2)(B)(i)(II)) DOE conducts this comparison in its LCC and PBP analyses.

The LCC is the sum of the purchase price of a product (including its installation) and the operating expense (including energy, maintenance, and repair expenditures) discounted over the lifetime of the product. The LCC analysis requires a variety of inputs, such as product prices, product energy consumption, energy prices, maintenance and repair costs, product lifetime, and consumer discount rates. To account for uncertainty and variability in specific inputs, such as product lifetime and discount rate, DOE uses a distribution of values, with probabilities attached to each value. For its analysis, DOE assumes that consumers will purchase the covered products in the first year of compliance with amended standards.

The PBP is the estimated amount of time (in years) it takes consumers to recover the increased purchase cost (including installation) of a more-efficient product through lower operating costs. DOE calculates the PBP by dividing the change in purchase cost due to a more-stringent standard by the change in annual operating cost for the year that standards are assumed to take effect.

The LCC savings for the considered energy conservation levels are calculated relative to a base case that reflects projected market trends in the absence of new or amended standards. DOE identifies the percentage of consumers estimated to receive LCC savings or experience an LCC increase, in addition to the average LCC savings associated with a particular standard level. In contrast, the PBP is measured relative to the baseline product. DOE's LCC and PBP analysis is discussed in further detail in section IV.F.

c. Energy Savings

Although significant conservation of energy is a separate statutory requirement for adopting an energy conservation standard, EPCA requires DOE, in determining the economic justification of a standard, to consider the total projected energy savings that are expected to result directly from the standard. (42 U.S.C. 6295(o)(2)(B)(i)(III)) As discussed in section IV.H, DOE uses the NIA spreadsheet to project national energy savings.

d. Lessening of Utility or Performance of Products

In establishing product classes and in evaluating design options and the impact of potential standard levels, DOE evaluates potential standards that would not lessen the utility or performance of the considered products. (42 U.S.C. 6295(o)(2)(B)(i)(IV))

Based on data available to DOE, the standards proposed in this notice would not reduce the utility or performance of the products under consideration in this rulemaking. DOE seeks comment regarding this tentative conclusion in Issue 4 of section VII.E "Issues on Which DOE Seeks Comment."

e. Impact of Any Lessening of Competition

EPCA directs DOE to consider the impact of any lessening of competition, as determined in writing by the Attorney General, that is likely to result from a proposed standard. (42 U.S.C. 6295(o)(2)(B)(i)(V)) It also directs the Attorney General to determine the impact, if any, of any lessening of competition likely to result from a proposed standard and to transmit such determination to the Secretary within 60 days of the publication of a proposed rule, together with an analysis of the nature and extent of the impact. (42 U.S.C. 6295(o)(2)(B)(ii)) DOE will transmit a copy of this proposed rule to the Attorney General with a request that the Department of Justice (DOJ) provide its determination on this issue. DOE will publish and respond to the Attorney General's determination in the final rule.

f. Need for National Energy Conservation

DOE also considers the need for national energy conservation in determining whether a new or amended standard is economically justified. (42 U.S.C. 6295(o)(2)(B)(i)(VI)) The energy savings from new or amended standards are likely to provide improvements to the security and reliability of the nation's energy system. Reductions in the demand for electricity also may result in reduced costs for maintaining the reliability of the nation's electricity system. DOE conducts a utility impact analysis to estimate how standards may affect the nation's needed power generation capacity, as discussed in section IV.M.

New or amended standards also are likely to result in environmental benefits in the form of reduced emissions of air pollutants and greenhouse gases associated with energy production. DOE conducts an emissions analysis to estimate how standards may affect these emissions, as discussed in section IV.K. DOE also estimates the economic value of emissions reductions resulting from the considered TSLs, as discussed in section IV.L.

g. Other Factors

EPCA allows the Secretary of Energy, in determining whether a standard is economically justified, to consider any other factors that the Secretary deems to be relevant. (42 U.S.C. 6295(o)(2)(B)(i)(VII)) To the extent interested parties submit any relevant information regarding economic justification that does not fit into the other categories described previously, DOE could consider such information under "other factors."

2. Rebuttable Presumption

As set forth in 42 U.S.C. 6295(o)(2)(B)(iii), EPCA creates a rebuttable presumption that an energy conservation standard is economically justified if the additional cost to the consumer of a product that meets the standard is less than three times the value of the first year's energy savings resulting from the standard, as calculated under the applicable DOE test procedure. DOE's LCC and PBP analyses generate values used to calculate the effects that proposed energy conservation standards would have on the payback period for consumers. These analyses include, but are not limited to, the 3-year payback period contemplated under the rebuttable-presumption test. In addition, DOE routinely conducts an economic analysis that considers the full range of impacts to consumers, manufacturers, the Nation, and the environment, as required under 42 U.S.C. 6295(o)(2)(B)(i). The results of this analysis serve as the basis for DOE's evaluation of the economic justification for a potential standard level (thereby supporting or rebutting the results of any preliminary determination of economic justification). The rebuttable presumption payback calculation is discussed in section V.B.1.c of this proposed rule.

H. Compliance Date

EPCA typically establishes a lead time between the publication of new or amended energy conservation standards and the date by which manufacturers must comply with that standard. As specifically relates to hearth products, EPCA requires that any new or amended standard for a consumer product which the Secretary classifies as a covered product under 42 U.S.C. 6292(b) shall not apply to products manufactured within five years after the publication of a final rule establishing such standard. (42 U.S.C. 6295(l)(2)) Accordingly, presuming DOE makes a final coverage determination, compliance with any standard for hearth products would be required five years after publication of the final rule.

I. Standby Mode and Off Mode

As discussed in section II.A of this NOPR, any final rule for amended or new energy conservation standards that is published on or after July 1, 2010 must address standby mode and off mode energy use. (42 U.S.C. 6295(gg)(3)) As previously stated, DOE considers the use of a continuously-burning pilot light to be standby mode energy consumption, and that disallowing use of the constant-burning pilot ignition systems would eliminate gas consumption for hearth products in standby mode.

In addition, DOE has tentatively determined that there is no off mode gas consumption for a hearth product's ignition module. As indicated in section III.B, this energy conservation standards rulemaking not only addresses but focuses on standby mode fossil fuel energy use.

DOE notes that in some instances, certain hearth product ignition modules may also have some ancillary electrical energy consumption in standby mode and/or off mode (see chapter 7 of the TSD). However, DOE has tentatively determined that such standby mode and off mode electrical energy consumption is *de minimis*, and consequently, DOE did not analyze energy conservation standards to regulate electrical standby mode and off mode energy consumption. DOE seeks comment on this assumption, which is identified as Issue 5 in section VII.E, "Issues on Which DOE Seeks Comment."

IV. Methodology

This section addresses the analyses DOE has performed for this rulemaking with regard to hearth products. Separate subsections will address each component of DOE's analyses.

DOE used three spreadsheet tools to estimate the impact of today's proposed standards. The first spreadsheet calculates LCCs and PBPs of potential standards. The second provides shipments forecasts and then calculates national energy savings and net present value impacts of potential standards. Finally, DOE assessed manufacturer impacts, largely through use of the Government Regulatory Impact Model (GRIM). All three spreadsheet tools are available online at the rulemaking portion of DOE's website: www1.eere.energy.gov/buildings/appliance_standards/product.aspx?productid=83.

Additionally, DOE estimated the impacts on utilities and the environment that would be likely to result from potential standards for hearth products. DOE used the most recent version of EIA's National Energy Modeling System (NEMS) for the utility and environmental analyses.[27] NEMS simulates the energy sector of the U.S. economy. EIA uses NEMS to prepare its Annual Energy Outlook, a widely-known energy forecast for the United States. NEMS offers a sophisticated picture of the effect of standards, because it accounts for the interactions between the various energy supply and demand sectors and the economy as a whole.

---

[27] For more information on NEMS, refer to the U.S. Department of Energy, Energy Information Administration documentation. A useful summary is National Energy Modeling System: An Overview, DOE/EIA-0581(2009) (October 2009) (Available at: http://www.eia.gov/oiaf/aeo/overview/).

A. Market and Technology Assessment

DOE develops information that provides an overall picture of the market for the products concerned, including the purpose of the products, the industry structure, manufacturers, market characteristics, and technologies used in the products. This activity includes both quantitative and qualitative assessments, based primarily on publicly-available information. The subjects addressed in the market and technology assessment for this hearth products rulemaking include: (1) a determination of the scope of the rulemaking and product classes; (2) manufacturers and industry structure; (3) quantities and types of products sold and offered for sale; (4) retail market trends; (5) regulatory and non-regulatory programs; and (6) technologies or design options that could improve the energy efficiency of the product(s) under examination. The key findings of DOE's market assessment are summarized below. See chapter 3 of the NOPR TSD for further discussion of the market and technology assessment.

1. Consideration of Products for Inclusion in This Rulemaking

In section III.A, DOE presented the scope of coverage for the rulemaking. Presently, hearth products are not covered consumer products. Section III.A discusses the scope and coverage for this rulemaking in the context of the notice of proposed coverage determination published in the Federal Register on December 31, 2013 (December 2013 NOPD). 78 FR 79638.

There is no statutory definition of "hearth product." In the December 2013 NOPD, DOE proposed to adopt a definition of hearth product that means a gas-fired appliance that simulates a solid-fueled fireplace or presents a flame pattern (for aesthetics or other purpose) and that may provide space heating directly to the space in which it is installed.

In the December 2013 NOPD, DOE provided examples of several common hearth product types that would be covered under the proposed definition, including vented decorative hearth products, vented heater hearth products, vented gas logs, gas stoves, outdoor hearth products, and vent-less hearth products. Id. For purposes of analysis, DOE separated hearth products into product groups. For more details on the product groups DOE used for its analysis, see chapter 5 of the NOPR TSD.

DOE recognizes that match-lit hearth products would be covered under the proposed definition for "hearth product.". However, since these products do not include a standing pilot ignition system, they would not be affected by the proposed prescriptive standard. Therefore, DOE did not include match-lit products in its analysis, and accordingly, the results of the analysis do not reflect impacts on match-lit products.

2. Product Classes

As discussed in section III.C, EPCA contains criteria that DOE follows when establishing product classes for setting different energy conservation standards for covered product types. (42 U.S.C. 6295(q)) DOE has tentatively concluded that, based

55

on the information presented in section III.C, separate hearth product classes are not necessary for the prescriptive design requirement disallowing the use of standing pilots that is proposed in this NOPR.

In comments on the December 2013 NOPD, HPBA stated that there is no basis to assume that a ban on standing pilot lights could reasonably be implemented for the diverse range of products at issue. (HPBA, No. 5 at p. 9) With regards to this comment as it applies to product classes, it is unclear why a prescriptive requirement banning standing pilots could not be implemented across hearth product types. As previously stated, DOE surveyed product literature, performed teardown analyses, and conducted manufacturer interviews which revealed that the key components of electronic ignitions are shared by multiple product types. DOE found that alternatives to constant-burning pilot lights, namely match-lit and electronic ignition, were offered on all types of hearth systems, and that some of the alternatives (specifically electronic ignitions) would meet the safety requirements of those local jurisdictions where such requirements apply. Such evidence supports the conclusion that alternatives to constant-burning pilot lights are technologically feasible across the broad range of hearth products on the market. However, DOE also found that the implementation of alternatives to a constant-burning pilot are not implemented uniformly across all hearth types, given their slightly different characteristics. Thus, alternatives could be relatively more or less expensive to implement depending on the type of hearth product.

As shown in the engineering analysis of section IV.C below, while the prescriptive requirement would apply to all hearth products without establishing classes, DOE chose to analyze the most common hearth styles separately to more accurately assess the potential impacts of imposing a prescriptive requirement that would disallow the use of standing pilot ignition systems.

3. Technology Assessment

In a technology assessment, DOE identifies technologies and designs that could be used to improve the energy efficiency or performance of covered equipment. For this NOPR, DOE conducted a technology assessment to identify technologies or designs that could reduce the fuel consumption of hearth products. DOE has summarized the technologies and designs identified in Table IV.1. DOE seeks comment on its list of available technologies to reduce fuel consumption for hearth products; this is identified as Issue 6 in section VII.E, "Issues on Which DOE Seeks Comment." See chapter 3 of the NOPR TSD for a detailed description of each technology option.

Table IV.1 Technologies DOE Considered for Hearth Products

Technology Option	Description
Air-to-fuel ratio	Change in air-to-fuel ratio to achieve fuel savings
Burner port design	Size, shape, and pattern of burner ports to reduce fuel consumption
Simulated log design	Log style or size that allows use of less fuel for flame pattern
Pan burner media/bead type	Sand, silica, or other media that achieves taller/more attractive flame with less fuel
Reflective walls and/or other components inside combustion zone	Increase apparent size of flames without requiring additional fuel input. Potentially allows for the use of burners with smaller inputs
Circulating blower	Circulate heated air more effectively
Electronic ignition	Removes need for continuous standing pilot

Condensing heat exchanger	Transfers more heat from flue gas into ambient air

After identifying all potential technology options for reducing the energy consumption of hearth products, DOE performed the screening analysis (see section IV.B of this NOPR and chapter 4 of the NOPR TSD) on these technologies to determine which could be considered further in the analysis and which should be eliminated.

During manufacturer interviews, DOE inquired about these technologies or design considerations with regard to their prevalence and potential to achieve energy savings. With regard to the air-to-fuel ratio, burner port design, simulated log design, pan burner media, or reflective components, manufacturers found that these options resulted in either immeasurable or negligible energy savings. DOE received several responses during its manufacturer interviews that the design considerations DOE listed would have little or no bearing on reducing the input needed to achieve the required flame pattern. Manufacturers also indicated that an energy conservation standard based on one or more of these design options may inhibit hearth product manufacturers from providing a variety of overall aesthetic options. For these reasons, DOE did not consider these design options in the screening analysis.

B. Screening Analysis

DOE uses the following four screening criteria to determine which technology options are suitable for further consideration in an energy conservation standards rulemaking:

1. Technological feasibility. DOE will consider technologies incorporated in commercial products or in working prototypes to be technologically feasible.

2. Practicability to manufacture, install, and service. If mass production and reliable installation and servicing of a technology in commercial products could be achieved on the scale necessary to serve the relevant market at the time of the compliance date of the standard, then DOE will consider that technology practicable to manufacture, install, and service.

3. Adverse impacts on product utility or product availability. If DOE determines a technology would have a significant adverse impact on the utility of the product to significant subgroups of consumers, or would result in the unavailability of any covered product type with performance characteristics (including reliability), features, sizes, capacities, and volumes that are substantially the same as products generally available in the United States at the time, it will not consider this technology further.

4. Adverse impacts on health or safety. If DOE determines that a technology would have significant adverse impacts on health or safety, it will not consider this technology further.

10 CFR part 430, subpart C, appendix A, 4(a)(4) and 5(b).

DOE considered several design options to assess their potential to reduce the fuel consumption of the products that are the subject of this rulemaking, both in active mode and in standby mode. In the end, three technology options were considered in the screening analysis: (1) electronic ignition; (2), condensing heat exchangers; and (3) circulating blowers. All technologies considered in the technology assessment are listed in Table IV.1.See chapter 3 of the NOPR TSD for a detailed description of each technology option.

DOE has tentatively concluded that the electronic ignition, condensing heat exchanger, and circulating blower would not be screened out by any of the four screening criteria listed above. DOE notes that these technologies are currently commercially available for hearth products as well as other residential products and commercial equipment, and that their use does not pose any significant health or safety hazard.

With regards to impact of the electronic ignition on product availability, DOE notes that an electronic ignition provides the same functionality as a millivolt standing pilot gas valve, specifically the ability to be used with a remote control or thermostat. DOE has also tentatively determined that electronic ignition components are available for a wide range of gas-fired equipment beyond hearth products, and that the ability of hearth manufacturers to comply with the standard will not be restricted for lack of available components.

DOE seeks comment regarding the tentative conclusions reached in its screening analysis including impacts on product availability or product utility. This is Issue 4 in section VII.E "Issues on Which DOE Seeks Comment."

C. Engineering Analysis

This engineering analysis determines the change in manufacturing cost of hearth products associated with a prescriptive design requirement that disallows the use of a standing pilot. This relationship between manufacturer selling price and reduced energy consumption serves as the basis for cost-benefit calculations for individual consumers, manufacturers, and the Nation. DOE has identified the following three methodologies to generate the manufacturing costs needed for the engineering analysis: (1) the design-option approach, which provides the incremental costs of adding to a baseline model design options that will improve its efficiency; (2) the efficiency-level approach, which provides the relative costs of achieving increases in energy efficiency levels, without regard to the particular design options used to achieve such increases; and (3) the cost-assessment (or reverse-engineering) approach, which provides "bottom-up" manufacturing cost assessments for both standing pilot models and electronic ignition models, based on detailed data as to costs for parts and material, labor, shipping/packaging, and investment.

For this NOPR, DOE conducted the engineering analysis for hearth products using a combination of the design-option approach and the cost-assessment approach. DOE selected hearth models that represented a range of hearth configurations (*e.g.*, vented fireplaces, vented fireplace inserts, unvented fireplace inserts, vented gas log sets, and unvented gas log sets). In light of the analytical focus on a prescriptive requirement for standby mode energy consumption (as discussed in section III.B) representative models were chosen that would allow a direct comparison between standing pilot and electronic ignition systems. DOE gathered additional information using reverse-engineering methodologies, product information from manufacturer catalogs and manuals, and discussions with manufacturers and other experts on hearth products.

DOE generated a bill of materials (BOM) by disassembling products representing a range of hearth configurations, including vented and unvented fireplaces, inserts, and stoves, vented and unvented gas log sets, and outdoor products. The BOMs describe the product in detail, including all manufacturing steps required to make and/or assemble each part. Subsequently, DOE developed a cost model that converted the BOMs into manufacturer production costs (MPCs). By applying derived manufacturer markups to the MPCs, DOE calculated the manufacturer selling prices.

DOE seeks comment on its general approach to the engineering analysis. This is Issue 7 in section VII.E, "Issues on Which DOE Seeks Comment." See chapter 5 of the NOPR TSD for additional details about the engineering analysis.

1. Representative Products for Analysis

For the engineering analysis, DOE reviewed the most common types of hearth products. Within each hearth type, DOE chose units for analysis that represent a cross-section of the hearth products market. As discussed in section IV.C.2 below, DOE eliminated the circulating blower and condensing heat exchanger technology options prior to the engineering analysis, since this rulemaking is focused on the standby mode energy use as described in section III.B. Consequently, the remaining technology – electronic ignition – became the main focus of DOE's analysis. DOE selected representative products for analysis that allowed DOE to determine whether any differences existed in ignition systems between hearth product types. DOE assumed that, should standing pilot ignitions be disallowed, manufacturers would convert standing pilot models to electronic ignition models rather than match-lit in order to provide the same level of safety, comfort, and functionality.

In order to inform the model selection process, DOE first surveyed product literature to determine whether clear differences in ignition systems existed between hearth products. Parts lists contained in installation and operation manuals for hearth products revealed that the key purchased components for electronic ignition systems – gas valves, pilot assemblies, and digital or analog control modules – are common across various hearth products, particularly for indoor fireplaces, fireplace inserts, stoves, and gas log sets. DOE also is aware that while gas log sets share these ignition components with other hearth product types, the nature of a gas log set (lacking a firebox or cabinet), means these components (particularly the gas valve and control module on electronic ignition systems) are more difficult to conceal. DOE seeks comment on the availability of these components and their applicability across hearth product configurations. This is identified as Issue 8 in section VII.E, "Issues on Which DOE Seeks Comment."

DOE selected units that represented the hearth configurations in Table IV.2.

Table IV.2 Representative Hearth Categories for Engineering Analysis

Hearth Product Analysis Category	Standing Pilot Valve	Electronic Ignition System
Vented Fireplaces, Inserts, and Stoves	Millivolt	Intermittent Pilot Ignition
	Millivolt	Intermittent Pilot Ignition
Unvented Fireplaces, Inserts, and Stoves	Millivolt	Intermittent Pilot Ignition
Vented Gas Log Sets	Manual	Intermittent Pilot Ignition
Unvented Gas Logs Sets	Manual	Intermittent Pilot Ignition
Outdoor Hearth Products	Manual	Intermittent Pilot Ignition (Hot Wire)
	Manual	Intermittent Pilot Ignition

As stated in section IV.A.2, DOE is aware of the industry claim that different hearth products serve different functions and differ in design. However, this engineering analysis is limited to a determination of the difference in manufacturer production cost between ignition styles (standing pilot and electronic ignition). DOE has tentatively determined that there is no difference in ignition components between various types of vented hearth products. DOE believes that the same gas valves, control modules, and pilot assemblies are used interchangeably between vented fireplaces, inserts, and stoves. Therefore, the engineering analysis determined one MPC that would apply globally to vented fireplaces, inserts, and stoves. DOE seeks comment on the assumption that vented fireplaces, inserts, and stoves are equivalent in terms of ignition component costs. This is identified as Issue 9 in section VII.E, "Issues on Which DOE Seeks Comment."

Unvented hearth products differ from their vented counterparts in several respects; with regards to the ignition components, unvented hearth products require an oxygen depletion sensor. The oxygen depletion sensor consists of a thermocouple and a precisely calibrated pilot light. DOE analyzed a separate unvented fireplace, insert, and stove category and an unvented gas log set category in order to account for any potential cost difference for these components.

In addition, DOE considered that there are two main standing pilot valve types: manual and millivolt. The manual valve requires the user to manually open and close the valve and is, therefore, smaller, simpler, and cheaper. The millivolt gas valve uses a thermopile to generate a voltage difference such that the valve can be coupled with additional control systems, for example a remote control or thermostat. Since gas log sets are subject to physical space constraints that fireplaces, inserts, and stoves are not, DOE selected gas log sets with manual valves as representative of gas log sets with standing pilots. DOE selected models with millivolt gas valves as being representative of the fireplace, insert and stove vented and unvented categories.

The pilot light on manual or millivolt valves may be ignited using a match or using a piezo-electric or battery-powered sparker. Because the standing pilot can be ignited manually without the use of a sparker, and because the function of the pilot is not affected by how it is initially lit, DOE does not consider this sparker an integral component to the ignition system for the purposes of this analysis. Therefore, DOE did not include these costs in its analysis of the cost of a standing pilot ignition.

2. Design Options Analyzed

As indicated in section III.B, in light of the greater energy savings possible from a design requirement disallowing standing pilot ignitions as opposed to a performance standard, this rulemaking is focused on standby mode energy consumption. However, two of the three technologies that passed the screening analysis in Section IV.B (the condensing heat exchanger and circulating fan) are technologies that affect the active mode energy consumption of a subset of hearth products. DOE therefore eliminated the condensing heat exchanger and circulating fan prior to conducting its engineering analysis. Rather, DOE focused its engineering analysis on the impacts of a prescriptive design requirement to remove the standing pilot ignition system and replace it with a system that does not use a continuously burning pilot.

For each of the representative products, DOE estimated manufacturer production costs for standing pilot ignitions and electronic ignitions. DOE has tentatively determined that the pilot light is a feature that can potentially be present on any type of hearth product and is the primary mode of energy consumption for those hearth products. Neither public comment nor the manufacturer interview process revealed additional design options that could replace a standing pilot or substantially reduce the fuel consumption of the pilot light, save for a match-lit burner. (However, a match-lit burner would not comply with the American National Standards Institute (ANSI) safety standards, and, thus, was not considered as a direct replacement for standing pilot ignition systems.) DOE has also tentatively concluded that a performance standard for standby mode as opposed to a design requirement would be impractical, since DOE found that there were no additional design options that would reduce the fuel consumption of a pilot light. In addition, a performance standard would increase burden on manufacturers, as it would require testing to demonstrate compliance with such standard.

As previously stated, hearth products currently are not covered products. They would become covered products should the December 2013 NOPD result in a positive final determination of coverage. Therefore, there is currently no minimum efficiency standard in place for DOE to use as a baseline for comparison. In terms of standby mode operation, DOE has tentatively determined that the standing pilot ignition system represents the baseline design in terms of energy consumption. A standing pilot consumes the most energy during standby mode operation; match-lit and intermittent pilots both represent reductions in energy consumption compared to the standing pilot.

DOE understands that in those jurisdictions where match-lit systems are permissible, and particularly for gas log sets, match-light remains a viable alternative to a standing pilot. A match-lit burner does not have an ignition system, and so DOE understands that the manufacturing cost of a match-lit burner is less than either a standing pilot or electronic ignition system. However, DOE recognizes that many jurisdictions require ANSI safety standard certification, and as such, a match-lit burner is not permissible. Since a match-lit system cannot serve as a replacement to current standing pilot models in these jurisdictions, electronic ignition would be the only viable alternative. The analysis, therefore, assumes that the representative change in cost for hearth products resulting from this proposed standard would be that associated with a change from a standing pilot to electronic ignition.

EPCA requires DOE to determine the maximum improvement in energy efficiency or maximum reduction in energy use that is technologically feasible for each class of covered products. (42 U.S.C. 6295(o)) As described previously (see section IV.A.2 and IV.B), none of the technologies identified by DOE to improve active mode efficiency could be applied to all hearth products, so DOE's analysis focused on reducing the standby mode energy consumption as providing the greatest opportunity for energy savings. In the case of a standing pilot, the maximum reduction in energy use possible is removal of the standing pilot entirely, and switching to either a match-lit or electronic ignition system. Both of these possibilities would be compliant with the proposed requirement to disallow the use of standing pilot ignition systems. This is the scenario DOE has chosen to analyze (see Table IV.2); as noted above, DOE is unaware of any other design options on the market that would substantially reduce the energy consumption of hearth products during standby operation.

3. Cost-Assessment Methodology

DOE identified intermittent pilot ignition as the relevant design option for reducing standing pilot energy consumption, as determined in the market assessment. Next, DOE selected products for the physical teardown analysis that represented the most common configurations of hearth products. DOE gathered the information from the physical teardown analysis to create bills of materials using a reverse engineering methodology. DOE then calculated the manufacturer production cost (MPC) for complete hearth products utilizing both design options, standing pilot and intermittent pilot ignition systems.

During the preparation and refining of the cost-efficiency comparison and MPCs for this NOPR, DOE also held interviews with manufacturers to gain insight into the hearth industry. DOE used the information gathered from these interviews, along with the information gathered through additional teardown analysis, to refine assumptions in the cost model. Next, DOE converted the MPCs into MSPs using publicly-available industry financial data, in addition to manufacturers' feedback. Further information on the analysis methodology is presented in subsections (a) through (g) of this section. For additional detail, see chapter 5 of the NOPR TSD.

a. Teardown Analysis

To assemble bills of materials (BOMs) and to calculate the manufacturing costs of the different components in hearth products, DOE disassembled several hearth products into their base components and estimated the materials, processes, and labor required for the manufacture of each individual component, a process referred to as a "physical teardown." Using the data gathered from the physical teardowns, DOE characterized each component according to its weight, dimensions, material, quantity, and the manufacturing processes used to fabricate and assemble it. The teardown analysis for this engineering analysis included 14 physical teardowns.

DOE used the teardown analysis to create detailed, structured BOMs for each hearth type or style. The BOMs incorporate all materials, components, and fasteners (classified as either raw materials or purchased parts and assemblies), and characterize the materials and components by weight, manufacturing processes used, dimensions, material, and quantity. The BOMs from the teardown analysis were then used as inputs placed into the cost model to calculate the MPC for the representative product for each product type and for each ignition type. See chapter 5 of the NOPR TSD for more details on the teardown analysis.

b. Cost Model

The cost model is a computer spreadsheet that converts the materials and components in the BOMs into dollar values based on the price of materials, average labor rates associated with manufacturing and assembling, and the cost of overhead and depreciation. To convert the information in the BOMs to dollar values for the NOPR analysis, DOE collected information on labor rates, tooling costs, raw material prices, and other factors. For purchased parts, the cost model estimates the purchase price based on volume-variable price quotations and discussions with manufacturers. For fabricated parts, the prices of raw metal materials (e.g., tube, sheet metal) are estimated on the basis of 5-year averages (from July 2009 to June 2014).[28] The cost of transforming the

intermediate materials into finished parts is estimated and confirmed through

manufacturer interviews. Chapter 5 of the NOPR TSD describes DOE's cost model and

definitions, assumptions, and estimates.

c. Manufacturing Production Cost

Once the cost estimate for each teardown unit was finalized, DOE totaled the cost

of materials, labor, and direct overhead used to manufacture a product in order to

calculate the manufacturer production cost for the NOPR. The total cost of the product

was broken down into two main costs: (1) the full manufacturer production cost or MPC;

and (2) the non-production cost, which includes selling, general, and administration

(SG&A) expenses; the cost of research and development; and interest from borrowing for

operations or capital expenditures. DOE estimated the MPC for both ignition designs

(*i.e.*, standing pilot and intermittent pilot). After DOE incorporates all of the assumptions

into the cost model, DOE calculates the different percentages of each aspect of

production cost (i.e. materials, labor, depreciation, and overhead) that make up the total

production cost. DOE uses these production cost percentages in the MIA (see section

IV.J).

---

[28] Raw material prices were obtained from American Metals Market (Available at: www.amm.com) (Last accessed June 2014).

d. Cost Comparison

The result of this engineering analysis is a typical MPC for a unit with standing pilot in each product group and the added incremental cost of converting a standing pilot ignition to an electronic ignition. DOE determined five of these MPCs and incremental costs, each corresponding to one of the five hearth product groups DOE selected for analysis. Section IV.C.4 of this NOPR and chapter 5 of the NOPR TSD contain the MPCs and incremental costs.

e. Manufacturer Markups

DOE uses MSPs to conduct its downstream economic analyses. DOE calculated the MSPs by multiplying the manufacturer production cost by a mark-up and adding the product's shipping cost. The production price of the product is marked up to ensure that manufacturers can make a profit on the sale of the equipment. DOE gathered information from manufacturer interviews to determine the mark-up used by different manufacturers. Using this information, DOE calculated an average mark-up of 1.45 for hearth products. DOE requests comments on the proposed mark-up, and this is identified as Issue 10 in section VII.E, "Issues on Which DOE Seeks Comment."

f. Manufacturer Interviews

Throughout the rulemaking process, DOE seeks feedback and insight from interested parties to improve the information used in its analyses. DOE interviewed manufacturers as a part of the NOPR manufacturer impact analysis (see section IV.J). During the confidential interviews, DOE sought feedback on all aspects of its analyses for hearth products. For the engineering analysis, DOE discussed the analytical assumptions, estimates, and purchased part prices with manufacturers. DOE considered all the information manufacturers provided when refining the cost model and assumptions. However, DOE incorporated equipment and manufacturing process figures into the analysis as averages in order to avoid disclosing sensitive information about individual manufacturers' products or manufacturing processes. More details about the manufacturer interviews are contained in chapter 12 of the NOPR TSD.

4. Results

The results from the engineering analysis are shown in Table IV.3. The cost model calculates an MPC for an associated annual production volume. As described in section IV.C.3.b, the cost model calculates manufacturer overhead and depreciation costs on a per-unit basis. Therefore, given the same number of employees, tooling, and equipment, a higher annual production volume will generally result in a lower MPC. Additionally, purchased parts scale non-linearly with volume: at low volumes, purchase part prices increase exponentially. Production volumes varied significantly across the segments of the hearth products industry. Replacing a standing pilot ignition system with an intermittent pilot ignition system largely means switching out one set of purchased part components with another. Purchased part component prices are dependent upon the volumes in which they are purchased, and as a result, the annual production volume for a given market segment could have a large impact on the cost of changing from a standing pilot ignition system to an intermittent pilot ignition system. As part of the confidential manufacturer interview process, DOE asked manufacturers to confirm costs and

73

quantities particularly for purchase parts associated with the ignition system. DOE notes

that this feedback is crucial in obtaining MPCs that accurately reflect typical industry

values. Accordingly, DOE is seeking further feedback on the derived MPCs found in

Table IV.3. This is Issue 10 in section VII.E, "Issues on Which DOE Seeks Comment."

Table IV.3 Estimated Typical Manufacturer Production Costs

Product Category	Representative Production Volume	Standing Pilot MPC	Added Electronic Ignition System (EIS) Cost
Vented Fireplaces, Inserts, Stoves	10,000	$322	$28
Unvented Fireplaces, Inserts, Stoves	2,000	$281	$32
Vented Gas Log Sets	2,000	$190	$70
Unvented Gas Log Sets	5,000	$208	$56
Outdoor	3,000	$210	$55

The "Standing Pilot MPC" represents the cost to the manufacturer of the complete

hearth product with a typical standing pilot ignition. The "Added EIS Cost" represents

the incremental cost to the manufacturer of replacing the standing pilot ignition

components with an electronic ignition. DOE has not included remote control or other

user control features as part of either ignition system. While DOE acknowledges many

electronic ignition systems are sold with a remote control and receiver, DOE does not

consider these components necessary to the intermittent function of the pilot light.

Therefore, DOE has not considered remote controls or remote control receivers in the

"Added EIS Cost."

The standing pilot MPC derived for vented fireplaces, inserts and stoves is higher than for unvented for several reasons. The representative models used for the vented category are direct vent. These units typically include a glass viewing pane with spring-loaded clamps holding the viewing pane in place. They also include blowers that regulate airflow and moderate surface temperatures so that the unit can be installed flush against combustible building materials. Again, DOE estimates that the MPC of similarly-sized vented units are the same. DOE makes this assumption because product advertising and literature and manuals indicated that key components to the ignitions systems are shared across product types and throughout industry.

In the case of gas log sets, the analysis used standing pilot models with manual gas valves. These valves are less expensive than millivolt gas valves, and so the difference between standing pilot and electronic ignition system is higher for gas log sets than for fireplaces, inserts, and stoves.

The results from the engineering analysis were used in the LCC analysis to determine consumer prices for hearth products using both design options, standing pilot and electronic ignition. Using the manufacturer markup, DOE calculated the MSPs of the representative hearth products from the MPCs developed using the cost model.

Again, DOE seeks comment on the MPCs estimated for hearth products and this is identified as Issue 10 in section VII.E "Issues on Which DOE Seeks Comment."

Chapter 5 of the NOPR TSD provides the full list of MPCs and MSPs for each analyzed representative product group.

D. Markups Analysis

DOE uses distribution channel markups (*e.g.*, manufacturer markups, retailer markups, distributor markups, contractor markups) and sales taxes (where appropriate) to convert the manufacturer production cost estimates from the engineering analysis to consumer prices, which are then used in the LCC and PBP analysis and in the manufacturer impact analysis. The markups are multipliers that are applied to the purchase cost at each stage in the distribution channel for hearth products. Before developing markups, DOE defines key market participants and identifies distribution channels.

DOE characterized two distribution channels to describe how hearth products pass from the manufacturer to consumers: (1) replacement market and (2) new construction. The replacement market channel is characterized as follows:

Manufacturer → Wholesaler → Mechanical contractor → Consumer

The new construction distribution channel is characterized as follows:

Manufacturer → Wholesaler → Mechanical contractor → General contractor → Consumer

The derivation of the manufacturer mark-up is discussed in section IV.C.3.e. To develop mark-ups for the parties involved in the distribution of the product, DOE utilized several sources, including: (1) the Heating, Air-Conditioning & Refrigeration Distributors International (HARDI) 2013 Profit Report[29] to develop wholesaler mark-ups; (2) the Air Conditioning Contractors of America's (ACCA) 2005 financial analysis for the heating, ventilation, air-conditioning, and refrigeration (HVACR) contracting industry[30] to develop mechanical contractor mark-ups, and (3) U.S. Census Bureau 2007 Economic Census data[31] for the residential and commercial building construction industry to develop general contractor mark-ups.

For wholesalers and contractors, DOE develops baseline and incremental mark-ups based on the product mark-ups at each step in the distribution chain. The baseline mark-up relates the change in the manufacturer selling price of baseline models to the change in the consumer purchase price. The incremental mark-up relates the change in the manufacturer selling price of higher-efficiency models (the incremental cost increase) to the change in the consumer purchase price.

In addition to the mark-ups, DOE derived State and local taxes from data provided by the Sales Tax Clearinghouse.[32] These data represent weighted-average taxes

---

[29] Heating, Air Conditioning & Refrigeration Distributors International 2013 Profit Report (Available at: http://www.hardinet.org/Profit-Report) (Last accessed April 10, 2013).
[30] Air Conditioning Contractors of America (ACCA), Financial Analysis for the HVACR Contracting Industry: 2005 (Available at: https://http://www.acca.org/store/product.php?pid=142) (Last accessed April 10, 2013).
[31] U.S. Census Bureau, 2007 Economic Census Data (Available at: http://www.census.gov/econ/)(Last accessed April 10, 2013).
[32] Sales Tax Clearinghouse Inc., State Sales Tax Rates Along with Combined Average City and County Rates, 2013 (Available at: http://thestc.com/STrates.stm) (Last accessed May 27, 2014).

that include county and city rates. DOE derived shipment-weighted-average tax values for each region considered in the analysis.

Chapter 6 of the NOPR TSD provides further detail on the estimation of markups.

E. Energy Use Analysis

The purpose of the energy use analysis is to determine the annual energy consumption of pilot lights in residential hearth products in use in the United States in representative homes and to assess the energy savings potential in switching from standing pilot lights to intermittent pilot lights. DOE used information from teardowns and manufacturer literature to establish a representative input capacity for each hearth product pilot light option. These input capacities are consistent with comments received from stakeholders during the previous rulemaking.[33] DOE estimated the annual energy consumption of hearth product pilot lights across a range of climate zones for a sample of houses that use hearth products. The annual energy consumption includes the natural gas used by the standing pilot or the electricity used by the intermittent pilot. The annual energy consumption of hearth product pilot lights is used in subsequent analyses, including the LCC and PBP analysis and the national impacts analysis.

The energy use analysis seeks to capture the range of operating conditions for hearth products in the field (i.e., as they are actually used by consumers). To determine the field energy use of hearth product pilot lights, DOE established a sample of households using hearth products from the Energy Information Administration's (EIA)

_____

[33] Docket Number EERE-2011-BT-STD-0047.

2009 Residential Energy Consumption Survey (RECS 2009).[34] DOE included in the sample all households who reported having a fireplace fueled by natural gas or liquefied petroleum gas (LPG).

DOE derived a range of possible operating hours for hearth products from field studies.[35,36] The hearth product operating hours for each household were sampled based on typical behavior patterns and household-specific characteristics, such as heating load, length of heating season, and primary heating appliance. DOE established three ranges that correspond to three modes of consumer behavior: (1) consumers who closely monitor the standing pilot light operation and only use it when starting the hearth product; (2) consumers who leave the standing pilot light on for the entirety of the heating season but turn it off for the remainder of the year; or (3) consumers who leave the standing pilot light on for the entire year. DOE represented each of these three modes with a continuous distribution of standing pilot operating hours. The field data suggest that more than half of natural gas-fired hearth product users leave the pilot on year round.

DOE used the household location data from RECS 2009 to establish the length of the heating season for each household by accounting for the National Oceanic and

---

[34] U.S. Department of Energy: Energy Information Administration, Residential Energy Consumption Survey: 2009 RECS Survey Data (2013) (Available at: http://www.eia.gov/consumption/residential/data/2009/) (Last accessed March, 2013).
[35] Hayden, A.C.S. Fireplace Pilots Take Gas Use Sky High. Home Energy Magazine (Jan. 1997). (Available at: http://www.homeenergy.org/show/article/nav/hvac/page/28/id/1264).
[36] Menkedick, John, Pam Hartford, Shawna Collins, Shawn Shumaker, and Darlene Wells, Hearth Products Meter Study (1995-1997), Rep. no. GRI-97/0298, Gas Research Institute (1997).

Atmospheric Administration (NOAA) weather data for that location.[37] To establish the maximum standing pilot operating hours during the heating season, DOE estimated the burner operating hours (BOH) of the hearth product from the annual space heating fuel use reported in RECS 2009. (Note that the pilot light remains on when the main burner is operating.)

RECS 2009 data also provided other information about the household that was used to further refine the analysis, such as primary heating appliance type, whether the hearth product was the primary heating appliance, fuel type of primary heating appliance, whether the hearth product was vented or vent-less, and whether the house has a chimney.

The pilot light operating hours, coupled with the data on fuel use per hour from the engineering analysis, allowed for the calculation of hearth products' pilot light annual energy usage. The average energy use of a hearth product's standing pilot is approximately 3.6 million Btu per year. To estimate the annual electricity used by an intermittent pilot, DOE used the representative burner input and the average duty cycle length to calculate the number of cycles, and a conservative estimate of 30 seconds on-time per ignition. DOE coupled the above value with the representative input of 50 W to derive electricity consumption. The average energy use of the intermittent pilot option is less than one kWh per year.

---

[37] National Oceanic and Atmospheric Administration, NNDC Climate Data Online (2009) (Available at: http://www7.ncdc.noaa.gov/CDO/CDODivisionalSelect.jsp) (Last accessed July 29, 2014).

In the RECS 2009 sample, 23 percent of households with hearth products used liquefied petroleum gas (LPG). Because LPG is a relatively expensive fuel, DOE understands that this subset of users closely monitors pilot light operation. Therefore, for households with LPG-fired hearth products, DOE assumed the pilot operating hours to be approximately equal to the hearth product BOH.

DOE seeks comment regarding its assumptions and methodology used in determining pilot light energy use and this is identified as Issue 11 in section VII.E "Issues on Which DOE Seeks Comment."

In evaluating the energy savings of the considered efficiency measure, DOE considered the heat input of the pilot light into the conditioned space. Eliminating the gas pilot would mean that some of the heat would not contribute to heating the home, which would mean that the main heating system would need to operate somewhat more, and the air conditioning system would operate slightly less in cases where the pilot is left on year-round. DOE based its analysis for vented hearth products on a report from the Canadian Centre for Housing Technology,[38] which quantified the fraction of energy consumed by the standing pilot light that is delivered into the conditioned space as useful heat. DOE used this study to estimate the ratio of energy consumed by the standing pilot light to the heat delivered to the conditioned space for each vented hearth product group. For unvented hearth products, DOE assumed that the majority of the heat from the pilot is

[38] Armstrong M.M., Swinton, M.C. and Szadkowski, F.,. Assessment of the Impact of a Natural Gas Fireplace on Heating Energy Consumption and Room Temperatures at the Canadian Centre for Housing Technology (March 31, 2010) Canada Mortgage and Housing Corporation (Available at: http://chic.cmhc-schl.gc.ca/uhtbin/cgisirsi.exe/?ps=Ey6u7UxnJz/CHIC/17510006/60/502/X).)

81

input into the space. For outdoor units, none of the energy consumed by the pilot is considered useful heat. The additional energy use of the heating system was calculated for each sample household based on its estimated heating load and heating equipment. The reduction in air conditioning energy use was calculated in a similar manner. Inclusion of the indirect effects on heating and cooling systems reduces the gross savings from eliminating the standing pilot by approximately 20 percent on average.

It is important to note that DOE is proposing a prescriptive standard to eliminate the use of standing pilots in hearth products. As such, it would only reduce standby energy use, and would have no effect on hearth products' active-mode energy consumption. Therefore, the standard, if adopted, would not be expected to affect consumer usage of the product, and, thus, no rebound effect was applied to the energy use of hearth products.

DOE projected that household weights and household characteristics in 2021, the first full year of compliance with any new energy conservation standards for hearth products, would be the same as in RECS 2009. To characterize future new homes, DOE used a subset of RECS 2009 homes that were built after 2000.

DOE adjusted the energy use estimated for 2009 to normalize for weather by using 10-year heating degree-day (HDD) data from NOAA for each geographical region.[39] Historical monthly HDD data from NOAA for each geographical region was used to disaggregate the total energy use into monthly amounts, which allows DOE to apply monthly energy prices in the LCC and PBP analysis. See chapter 7 in the NOPR TSD for additional detail on the energy analysis for hearth product ignition devices.

DOE requests comment on the extent of assumed pilot light usage, specifically the percentages of consumers who operate their hearth product's standing pilot: (a) year-round; (b) during the heating season; and (c) only when operating the unit. DOE also requests comment on the pilot operating hours of LPG-fired hearth products and determination of heat input from the pilot light into the conditioned space. This is Issue 12 in section VII.E, "Issues on Which DOE Seeks Comment."

F. Life-Cycle Cost and Payback Period Analysis

In determining whether an energy conservation standard is economically justified, DOE considers the economic impact of potential standards on consumers. The effect of new or amended standards on individual consumers usually includes a reduction in operating cost and an increase in purchase cost. DOE used the following two metrics to measure consumer impacts:

- LCC (life-cycle cost) is the total consumer cost of an appliance or product, generally over the life of the appliance or product. The LCC calculation includes

---

[39] National Oceanic and Atmospheric Administration, NNDC Climate Data Online (2009) (Available at: http://www7.ncdc.noaa.gov/CDO/CDODivisionalSelect.jsp) (Last accessed July 29, 2014).

total installed cost (manufacturer selling price, distribution chain markups, sales tax, and installation costs), operating costs (energy, repair, and maintenance costs), equipment lifetime, and discount rate. Future operating costs are discounted to the time of purchase and summed over the lifetime of the appliance or product.

- PBP (payback period) measures the amount of time it takes consumers to recover the assumed higher purchase price of a more energy-efficient product through reduced operating costs. Inputs to the payback period calculation include the installed cost to the consumer and the first-year operating costs.

DOE analyzed the net effect of potential hearth product standards on consumers by calculating the LCC and PBP for each household for each considered pilot option. DOE measured the PBP and the change in LCC when switching from standing pilot to intermittent pilot in each hearth product type.

DOE performed the LCC and PBP analysis using a spreadsheet model combined with Crystal Ball (a commercially-available software program used to conduct stochastic analysis using Monte Carlo simulation and probability distributions) to account for uncertainty and variability among the input variables (e.g., energy prices, installation cost, and repair and maintenance costs). It uses weighting factors to account for distributions of shipments to different building types and States to generate LCC savings by potential standard level. Each Monte Carlo simulation consists of 10,000 LCC and PBP calculations using input values that are either sampled from probability distributions and household samples or characterized with single point values. The analytical results include a distribution of 10,000 data points showing the range of LCC savings and PBPs for a given standards level relative to the base-case forecast (*i.e.*, without new energy conservation standards). In performing an iteration of the Monte Carlo simulation for a given consumer, the probability that a hearth product type and pilot option is chosen is based on the existing market share. If the chosen pilot light for the consumer is intermittent, the LCC calculation reveals that a consumer is not impacted by the standard level. Similarly, for those consumers who diligently operate their standing pilot lights, the LCC calculation results in either a net cost or no impact, depending on the specific simulation round. By accounting for consumers who already purchase more-efficient products or operate their units efficiently, DOE avoids overstating the potential benefits from increasing product energy conservation.

EPCA establishes a rebuttable presumption that a standard is economically justified if the Secretary finds that the additional cost to the consumer of purchasing a product complying with an energy conservation standard level will be less than three times the value of the energy (and, as applicable, water) savings during the first year that the consumer will receive as a result of the standard, as calculated under the test procedure in place for that standard. (42 U.S.C. 6295(o)(2)(B)(iii)) DOE determines the value of the first year's energy savings by calculating the quantity of those savings in accordance with the applicable DOE test procedure and multiplying that amount by the average energy price forecast for the year in which compliance with the amended standards would be required. Since there is no DOE test procedure for hearth products,

DOE based its rebuttable pay back analysis on the average energy use and costs calculated in the LCC analysis.

As discussed in section IV.E, DOE developed nationally representative household samples from 2009 RECS. For each sampled household, DOE determined the energy consumption of the hearth product pilot light and the appropriate energy prices in the area where the household is located.

DOE calculated the LCC and PBP for all hearth product consumers as if each were to purchase the product in the year that compliance with amended standards is required. At the time of preparation of the NOPR analysis, the expected issuance date for the final rule was in December 2015. For newly-covered products, EPCA prescribes a five-year period between the standard's publication date and the compliance date (42 U.S.C. 6295(l)(2)), which leads to a compliance date in December 2020. For purposes of its analysis, DOE modeled hearth products purchased on or after this date as if they operated for a full year beginning on January 1, 2021 and continuing thereafter.

As noted above, DOE's LCC and PBP analyses generate values that calculate the payback period for consumers of potential energy conservation standards, which includes, but is not limited to, the three-year payback period contemplated under the rebuttable presumption test. However, DOE routinely conducts a full economic analysis that considers the full range of impacts, including those to the consumer, manufacturer, Nation, and environment, as required under 42 U.S.C. 6295(o)(2)(B)(i). The results of this analysis serve as the basis for DOE to definitively evaluate the economic justification for a potential standard level (thereby supporting or rebutting the results of any preliminary determination of economic justification).

1. Installed Cost

The primary inputs for establishing the total installed cost are the baseline consumer product price, standard-level consumer price increases, and installation costs (labor and material cost). Baseline consumer prices and standard-level consumer price increases were determined by applying mark-ups to manufacturer selling price estimates, including sales tax where appropriate. The installation cost is added to the consumer price to arrive at a total installed cost.

DOE found that the historic real (i.e., adjusted for inflation) producer price index (PPI) for floor and wall furnaces, unit heaters, infrared heaters, and mechanical stokers from 1999 to 2013 has been relatively flat.[40] Hearth products are generally similar to the products in this PPI. In the absence of any data indicating a trend in hearth product prices, DOE elected to use a constant future price trend. DOE requests feedback on the assumption of a constant future price trend for hearth products. This is identified as Issue 13 in section VII.E, "Issues on Which DOE Seeks Comment."

Because the pilot light is a component of the hearth product, the installation costs for most installations was $0. In a fraction of installations, the intermittent pilot could

---

[40] Series ID: PCU3334143334147 (Available at: http://www.bls.gov/ppi/).

87

necessitate an electrical connection, although many intermittent pilots are battery powered, and many hearth products already have electrical connections. For the cases where a new electrical connection is needed, DOE assumed a percentage of these needed electrical connection retrofits, with the probability increasing the older the house is. Similar assumptions were made for electrical grounding. For these cases needing retrofits, labor and material information was obtained from RS Means 2013 Residential Cost Data.[41] DOE requests feedback on the installation and retrofit assumptions regarding electrical connections and grounding. This is identified as Issue 14 in section VII.E, "Issues on Which DOE Seeks Comment."

2. Inputs to Operating Costs

The primary inputs for calculating the operating costs are product energy consumption, product efficiency, energy prices and forecasts, maintenance and repair costs, product lifetime, and discount rates. DOE uses discount rates to determine the present value of lifetime operating expenses. The discount rate used in the LCC analysis represents the rate from an individual consumer's perspective. Much of the data used for determining consumer discount rates comes from the Federal Reserve Board's triennial Survey of Consumer Finances.[42]

---

[41] RS Means Company Inc., RS Means Residential Cost Data (2013) (Available at: http://rsmeans.reedconstructiondata.com/).
[42] Available at www.federalreserve.gov/econresdata/scf/scfindex.htm.

a. Energy Consumption

For each sample household, DOE determined the energy consumption for the hearth product ignition devices using the approach described in section IV.E. As noted previously, because the proposed standard concentrates on reduction in standby mode energy consumption, DOE does not anticipate a rebound effect in terms of consumer usage.

b. Energy Prices

Using the most current data from EIA on average energy prices in various States and regions,[43,44,45] DOE assigned an appropriate energy price to each household in the sample, depending on its location (see chapter 8 of the NOPR TSD for details). Average electricity and natural gas prices from the EIA data were adjusted using seasonal marginal price factors to derive monthly marginal electricity and natural gas prices. For a detailed discussion of the development of marginal energy price factors, see appendix 8-C of the NOPR TSD.

To estimate future prices, DOE used the projected annual changes in average residential natural gas, LPG, and electricity prices in the Reference case projection in AEO 2014.

[43] U.S. Department of Energy-Energy Information Administration, Form EIA-826 Database Monthly Electric Utility Sales and Revenue Data (2013) (Available at: http://www.eia.doe.gov/cneaf/electricity/page/eia826.html).

[44] U.S. Department of Energy-Energy Information Administration, Natural Gas Navigator (2013) (Available at: http://tonto.eia.doe.gov/dnav/ng/ng_pri_sum_dcu_nus_m.htm).

[45] U.S. Department of Energy-Energy Information Administration, 2012 State Energy Consumption, Price, and Expenditure Estimates (SEDS) (2013) (Available at: http://www.eia.doe.gov/emeu/states/_seds.html).

c. Maintenance and Repair Costs

Repair costs are associated with repairing or replacing components in the hearth product that have failed, whereas maintenance costs are routine annual costs associated with maintaining the proper operation of the equipment. DOE's review of product literature suggests that that no maintenance is required for the ignition device. DOE estimated that a 7 percent failure rate for ignition systems in hearth products based on repair rates for residential furnace ignition systems.[46] DOE estimated separate repair costs for each ignition system option as a function of the manufacturer price estimated in the engineering analysis (section IV.C). Due to the increased price of the intermittent pilot, the cost of repairing these units was approximately 44 percent higher than for units with standing pilots. See chapter 8 of the NOPR TSD for details. DOE requests feedback on the repair cost assumptions. This is identified as Issue 15 in section VII.E, "Issues on Which DOE Seeks Comment."

d. Product Lifetime

Product lifetime is the age at which an appliance is retired from service. DOE assumed that the lifetime of the ignition device is identical to the lifetime of the hearth product. DOE conducted an analysis of hearth product lifetimes using a combination of data on shipments and the hearth product stock (see section IV.G) and RECS 2009 data on the age of the hearth products in homes. The data allowed DOE to develop a survival function, which provides a range from minimum to maximum lifetime, as well as an

---

[46] Jakob, F. E., J. J. Crisafulli, J. R. Menkedick, R. D. Fischer, D. B. Philips, R. L. Osbone, J. C. Cross, G. R. Whitacre, J. G. Murray, W. J. Sheppard, D. W. DeWirth, and W. H. Thrasher, Assessment of Technology for Improving the Efficiency of Residential Gas Furnaces and Boilers, Volume I and II—Appendices (September 1994) Gas Research Institute. AGA Laboratories. Report No. GRI–94/0175.

average lifetime. The average lifetime estimated for hearth products is 16 years. Chapter 8 of the NOPR TSD provides further details on the methodology and sources DOE used to develop hearth product lifetimes. DOE requests feedback on the lifetime assumptions. This is identified as Issue 16 in section VII.E, "Issues on Which DOE Seeks Comment."

e. Discount Rates

In the calculation of LCC, DOE applies discount rates to estimate the present value of future operating costs. The discount rate used in the LCC analysis represents the rate from an individual consumer's perspective.

To establish discount rates for consumers, DOE's approach involved identifying all relevant household debt or asset classes in order to approximate a consumer's opportunity cost of funds related to appliance energy cost savings and maintenance costs. It estimated the average percentage shares of the various types of debt and equity by household income group using data from the Federal Reserve Board's Survey of Consumer Finances (SCF) for 1995, 1998, 2001, 2004, 2007, and 2010.[47] Using the SCF and other sources, DOE then developed a distribution of rates for each type of debt and asset by income group to represent the rates that may apply in the year in which amended standards would take effect. DOE assigned each sample household a specific discount rate drawn from one of the distributions. The average rate across all types of household debt and equity and income groups, weighted by the shares of each class, is 4.2 percent.

---

[47] The Federal Reserve Board, Survey of Consumer Finances 1989, 1992, 1995, 1998, 2001, 2004, 2007, 2010 (Available at: http://www.federalreserve.gov/pubs/oss/oss2/scfindex.html).

See chapter 8 in the NOPR TSD for further details on the development of discount rates for the LCC analysis.

f. Base-Case Efficiency Distribution

To estimate the share of consumers affected by a potential energy conservation standard, DOE's LCC and PBP analysis considers the projected distribution (i.e., market shares) of product efficiencies that consumers will purchase in the first compliance year in the base case (i.e., the case without amended energy conservation standards).

For each of the hearth product groups, DOE estimated current market shares of the two pilot system types based on model information and manufacturer interviews. Because there are no data indicating trends in the market shares, DOE used the current shares to represent the market in 2021 (see Table IV.4).

Table IV.4 Base-Case Efficiency Distribution for Hearth Product Groups in 2021

Product Group	Pilot System Market Share	
	Standing Pilot	Intermittent Pilot
Vented Fireplaces, Inserts, Stoves	42%	58%
Unvented Fireplaces, Inserts, Stoves	88%	12%
Vented Gas Log Sets	87%	13%
Unvented Gas Log Sets	94%	6%
Outdoor	52%	48%

For further information on DOE's estimation of the base-case efficiency distributions for hearth products, see chapter 8 of the NOPR TSD. DOE requests feedback on the base-case efficiency distribution. This is identified as Issue 17 in section VII.E, "Issues on Which DOE Seeks Comment."

3. Inputs to Payback Period Analysis

The PBP is the amount of time it takes the consumer to recover the additional installed cost of more-efficient products, compared to baseline products, through energy cost savings. The simple PBP does not account for changes in operating expense over time or the time value of money. Payback periods are expressed in years. Payback periods that exceed the life of the product mean that the increase in total installed cost is not recovered in reduced operating expenses.

The inputs to the PBP calculation are the total installed cost of the product to the customer for each efficiency level and the average annual operating expenditures for each efficiency level. The PBP calculation uses the same inputs as the LCC analysis, except that discount rates are not needed.

EPCA establishes a rebuttable presumption that a standard is economically justified if the Secretary finds that the additional cost to the consumer of purchasing a product complying with an energy conservation standard level will be less than three times the value of the energy (and, as applicable, water) savings during the first year that the consumer will receive as a result of the standard, as calculated under the test procedure in place for that standard. (42 U.S.C. 6295(o)(2)(B)(iii)) For each considered standard level, DOE determined the value of the first year's energy savings by calculating the quantity of those savings in accordance with the applicable DOE test procedure and multiplying that amount by the average energy price forecast for the year in which compliance with the amended standard would be required.

The results of DOE's PBP analysis are presented in section V.B.1.

G. Shipments Analysis

DOE uses forecasts of product shipments to calculate the national impacts of potential new or amended energy conservation standards on energy use, NPV, and future manufacturer cash flows. Historical data indicate that shipments of hearth products are very sensitive to overall economic activity. Because DOE observed a strong correlation between housing starts and hearth product shipments, it used a 10-year average of the ratio of hearth product shipments to housing starts, along with the forecasted housing starts from AEO 2014, to project future hearth product shipments.

To estimate the impact of the considered standard on future hearth product shipments, DOE applied the same product price elasticity as it has used in many previous rulemakings for consumer products (see chapter 9 of the NOPR TSD). This elasticity relates an incremental increase in the price of hearth products to a decrease in shipments.

Regarding the potential for consumers to switch to other products, DOE recognizes that hearth products are purchased for the convenience of natural gas as a fuel source (as opposed to wood) and realistic flame characteristics (relative to electric-powered units). For this reason, DOE assumed that fuel switching among these products due to the imposition of the design standard would be negligible. DOE requests comment on this assumption, and this is identified as Issue 18 in Section VII.E, "Issues on Which DOE Seeks Comment."

DOE requests feedback on the methodology for hearth product shipment projections. This is identified as Issue 19 in section VII.E, "Issues on Which DOE Seeks Comment." For details on the shipments analysis, see chapter 9 of the NOPR TSD.

H. National Impact Analysis

The NIA assesses the national energy savings (NES) and the net present value (NPV) from a national perspective of total consumer costs and savings expected to result from new or amended energy conservation standards at specific efficiency levels. DOE determined the NPV and NES for the potential standard levels considered for the hearth product types analyzed.

To make the analysis more accessible and transparent to all interested parties, DOE used a computer spreadsheet model (as opposed to probability distributions) to calculate the energy savings and the national consumer costs and savings from each TSL.[48] The NIA calculations are based on the annual energy consumption and total installed cost data from the energy use analysis and the LCC analysis. In the NIA, DOE forecasted the lifetime energy savings, energy cost savings, installed product costs, and

---

[48] DOE's use of spreadsheet models provides interested parties with access to the models within a familiar context. In addition, the TSD and other documentation that DOE provides during the rulemaking help explain the models and how to use them, and interested parties can review DOE's analyses by changing various input quantities within the spreadsheet.

NPV of consumer benefits over the lifetime of hearth products sold from 2021 through 2050.

A key component of the NIA is the trend in energy efficiency forecasted for the base case (without new or amended standards) and each of the standards cases. Section IV.F.2.f describes how DOE developed a base-case energy efficiency distribution for hearth products for the first full year of compliance (2021). DOE projected base-case efficiency assuming a constant efficiency distribution over the 30-year period. Historical trends of data for this product are not available, especially regarding the necessary ignition details. Therefore, DOE has estimated current standing pilot shipments and assumed those would be constant during the 30-year period starting from compliance (2021-2050).

To estimate the impact that energy conservation standards for hearth products (i.e., a design requirement) may have in the year compliance becomes required, DOE used a "roll-up" scenario: (1) products with efficiencies in the base case that do not meet a potential standard level would "roll up" to meet that standard level, and (2) products at efficiencies above the standard level under consideration would not be affected. After the year of compliance, all hearth products would utilize electronic ignition devices. For further details about the NIA efficiency distributions, see chapter 10 of the NOPR TSD.

1. National Energy Savings

To develop the NES, DOE calculates annual energy consumption of the considered products for the base case and then compares that to each potential standards case (TSL). DOE calculates the annual energy consumption for each case using the appropriate per-unit annual energy use data multiplied by the projected hearth product shipments for each year. As explained in section IV.E, DOE did not include a rebound effect for hearth products.

To estimate the national energy savings expected from appliance standards, DOE used a multiplicative factor to convert site electricity consumption (at the home) into primary energy consumption (the energy required to convert and deliver the site electricity). These conversion factors account for the energy used at power plants to generate electricity. The factors vary over time due to changes in generation sources (i.e., the power plant types projected to provide electricity to the country) projected in AEO 2014. The factors that DOE developed are marginal values, which represent the response of the electricity sector to an incremental decrease in consumption associated with potential appliance standards. Cumulative energy savings are the sum of the NES for each year over the timeframe of the analysis.

In response to the recommendations of a committee on "Point-of-Use and Full-Fuel-Cycle Measurement Approaches to Energy Efficiency Standards" appointed by the National Academy of Sciences, DOE announced its intention to use full-fuel-cycle (FFC) measures of energy use and greenhouse gas and other emissions in the national impact analyses and emissions analyses included in future energy conservation standards rulemakings. 76 FR 51281 (August 18, 2011). After evaluating the approaches discussed in the August 18, 2011 notice, DOE published a statement of amended policy in the Federal Register in which DOE explained its determination that NEMS is the most appropriate tool for its FFC analysis and its intention to use NEMS for that purpose. 77 FR 49701 (August 17, 2012). The FFC factors incorporate losses in production and delivery in the case of natural gas (including fugitive emissions) and energy used to produce and deliver the fuels used by power plants. The approach used for this NOPR is described in appendix 10-B of the NOPR TSD.

2. Net Present Value of Consumer Benefit

The inputs for determining NPV are: (1) total annual installed cost; (2) total annual savings in operating costs; (3) a discount factor to calculate the present value of costs and savings; (4) present value of costs; and (5) present value of savings. To develop the national NPV of consumer benefits from potential energy conservation standards, DOE calculates annual operating costs (energy costs and repair and maintenance costs) and annual installed costs for the base case and the standards cases. DOE calculates annual energy expenditures from annual energy consumption using forecasted energy prices in each year. DOE calculates annual product expenditures by multiplying the price per unit times the projected shipments in each year. As discussed in section IV.F.1, DOE assumed a constant future product price trend.

The aggregate difference each year between operating cost savings and increased installed costs is the net savings. DOE multiplies the net savings in future years by a discount factor to determine their present value. DOE estimates the NPV of consumer benefits using both a 3-percent and a 7-percent real discount rate, in accordance with guidance provided by the Office of Management and Budget (OMB) to Federal agencies on the development of regulatory analysis.[49] The 7-percent real value is an estimate of the average before-tax rate of return to private capital in the U.S. economy. It approximates the opportunity cost of capital, and it is the appropriate discount rate whenever the main effect of a regulation is to displace or alter the use of capital in the private sector. Circular A-4 also states that when the regulation primarily and directly affects private consumption, a lower discount rate is appropriate. The 3-percent real value represents the "societal rate of time preference," which is the rate at which society discounts future consumption flows to their present value. If one takes the rate that the average saver uses to discount future consumption as a measure of the social rate of time preference, then the real rate of return on long-term government debt may provide a fair approximation. Over the last thirty years, the rate has averaged around 3 percent in real terms on a pre-tax basis. Energy conservation standards for appliances and equipment affect both the use of capital and private consumption. It is noted that the discount rates for the determination of NPV are in contrast to the discount rates used in the LCC analysis, which are designed to reflect a consumer's perspective.

---

[49] OMB Circular A-4, section E, "Identifying and Measuring Benefits and Costs" (Sept. 17, 2003) (Available at: http://www.whitehouse.gov/omb/memoranda/m03-21.html).

I. Consumer Subgroup Analysis

In analyzing the potential impacts of new or amended standards on consumers, DOE evaluated the impacts on identifiable subgroups of consumers that may be disproportionately affected by a national standard. The purpose of a subgroup analysis is to determine the extent of any such disproportional impacts. For this NOPR, DOE evaluated impacts of potential standards on two subgroups: (1) senior households and (2) low-income households. The subgroup samples were identified from RECS 2009 data on income and age of household members. DOE used the LCC and PBP spreadsheet model to analyze the LCC impacts and PBP for those particular consumers at the considered standard. The consumer subgroup results for the hearth products TSL are presented in section V.B.1.b of this notice and in chapter 11 of the NOPR TSD.

J. Manufacturer Impact Analysis

1. Overview

DOE performed a Manufacturer Impact Analysis (MIA) to estimate the financial impact of an energy conservation standard on manufacturers of gas hearth products and to calculate the potential impact of such standards on employment and manufacturing capacity. The MIA has both quantitative and qualitative aspects. The quantitative part of the MIA primarily relies on the Government Regulatory Impact Model (GRIM), an industry cash-flow model with inputs specific to this rulemaking. The key GRIM inputs are data on the industry cost structure, product costs, shipments, and assumptions about markups and conversion expenditures. The key output is the industry net present value (INPV). DOE used the GRIM to calculate cash flows using standard accounting principles and to compare changes in the INPV between a base case and each TSL (the standards case). The difference in INPV between the base case and a standards case represents the financial impact of energy conservation standards on gas hearth product manufacturers. DOE used different sets of assumptions (markup scenarios) to represent the uncertainty surrounding potential impacts on prices and manufacturer profitability as a result of standards. Different sets of assumptions will produce a range of INPV results. The qualitative part of the MIA addresses the proposed standard's potential impacts on manufacturing capacity and industry competition, as well as factors such as product characteristics, impacts on particular subgroups of firms, and important market and product trends. The complete MIA is outlined in chapter 12 of the NOPR TSD.

DOE conducted the MIA for this rulemaking in three phases. In Phase 1 of the MIA, DOE prepared a profile of the gas hearth industry. This industry characterization was based on the market and technology assessment, preliminary manufacturer interviews, and publicly-available information. Specifically, DOE developed its industry profile using a combination of sources, including public information, such as Securities and Exchange Commission (SEC) 10-K reports,[50] market research tools (*e.g.*, Hoovers[51]), corporate annual reports, the U.S. Census Bureau's 2011 Annual Survey of Manufacturers (ASM),[52] and the 2010 Energy Conservation Standard Final Rule for Residential Water Heaters, Direct Heating Equipment, and Pool Heaters (75 FR 20112

---

[50] U.S. Securities and Exchange Commission, Annual 10-K Reports (Various Years) (Available at: www.sec.gov).

[51] Hoovers Inc., Company Profiles, Various Companies (Available at: www.hoovers.com/).

[52] U.S. Census Bureau, Annual Survey of Manufacturers: General Statistics: Statistics for Industry Groups and Industries (2011) (Available at: http://www.census.gov/manufacturing/asm/index.html).

(April 16, 2010)); information obtained through DOE's engineering analysis, life-cycle cost analysis, and market and technology assessment prepared for this rulemaking; and information obtained directly from manufacturers through interviews.

As part of Phase 1, DOE conducted structured, detailed interviews with a representative cross-section of manufacturers. During these interviews, DOE discussed engineering, manufacturing, procurement, and financial topics to identify key issues or concerns and to inform and validate assumptions used in the GRIM. The industry profile developed as a result of Phase 1 research and interviews includes: (1) further detail on the overall market and product characteristics; (2) financial parameters such as net plant, property, and equipment; selling, general and administrative (SG&A) expenses; research and development (R&D) expenses; cost of goods sold; and tax rates; and (3) trends in the number of firms, market, and product characteristics.

In Phase 2 of the MIA, DOE prepared an industry cash-flow analysis to quantify the potential impacts of an energy conservation standard on manufacturers of gas hearth products. In general, energy conservation standards can affect manufacturer cash flow in three distinct ways: (1) create a need for increased investment; (2) raise production costs per unit; and (3) alter revenue due to higher per-unit prices and/or possible changes in sales volumes. To quantify these impacts, DOE used the GRIM to perform a cash-flow analysis for the gas hearth industry using financial values derived during Phase 1 and the shipment scenario used in the NIA.

In Phase 3 of the MIA, DOE evaluated subgroups of manufacturers that may be disproportionately impacted by energy conservation standards or that may not be represented accurately by the average cost assumptions used to develop the industry cash-flow analysis. For example, small manufacturers, niche players, or manufacturers exhibiting a cost structure that largely differs from the industry average could be more negatively affected. DOE identified two subgroups for separate impact analyses: (1) manufacturers of gas log sets; and (2) small businesses. The subgroup of gas log set manufacturers is discussed in section V.B.2.d of this notice, "Impacts on Subgroups of Manufacturers," and the small manufacturer subgroup is discussed in section VI.B, "Review Under the Regulatory Flexibility Act." Impacts on both subgroups are also addressed in chapter 12 of the NOPR TSD.

2. Government Regulatory Impact Model

DOE uses the GRIM to quantify changes in cash flow due to new standards that result in a higher or lower industry value. The GRIM uses a standard, annual cash-flow analysis using standard accounting principles that incorporates manufacturer costs, markups, shipments, and industry financial information as inputs. The GRIM models changes in costs, distribution of shipments, investments, and manufacturer margins that could result from a potential energy conservation standard. The GRIM spreadsheet uses the inputs to arrive at a series of annual cash flows, beginning in 2014 (the base year of the analysis) and continuing to 2050. Manufacturers incur capital and product conversion costs in the period between the date at which the rule is promulgated and the compliance date of an amended standard. To capture the impacts of these expenditures on industry

103

finances, the MIA analysis period begins before the compliance year. DOE calculated INPVs by summing the stream of annual discounted cash flows during this period. For gas hearth manufacturers, DOE used a real discount rate of 8.7 percent, which was derived from industry financial information and then modified according to feedback received during manufacturer interviews.

After calculating industry cash flows and INPV, DOE compared changes in INPV between the base case and the standards case. The difference in INPV between the base case and the standards case represents the financial impact of that potential energy conservation standard on manufacturers. As discussed previously, DOE collected information on key GRIM inputs from a number of sources, including publicly-available data and confidential interviews with manufacturers (described in the next section). The GRIM results are shown in section V.B.2. Additional details about the GRIM, the discount rate, and other financial parameters can be found in chapter 12 of the NOPR TSD.

a. Government Regulatory Impact Model Key Inputs

Manufacturer Production Costs

Manufacturing a higher-efficiency product is typically more expensive than manufacturing a baseline product due to the use of more complex components, which are typically more costly than baseline components. The changes in the manufacturer production costs (MPCs) of the analyzed products can affect the revenues, gross margins, and cash flow of the industry, making these equipment cost data key GRIM inputs for DOE's analysis.

In the MIA, DOE used the MPCs calculated in the engineering analysis, as described in section IV.C and further detailed in chapter 5 of the NOPR TSD. In addition, DOE used information from its teardown analysis, described in chapter 5 of the TSD, to disaggregate the MPCs into material, labor, and overhead costs. These costs were shared with manufacturers and revised to incorporate their feedback.

Shipments Forecasts

The GRIM estimates manufacturer revenues based on total unit shipment forecasts and the distribution of these values by product group and ignition type. Changes in sales volumes and product mix over time can significantly affect manufacturer finances. For this analysis, the GRIM uses the NIA's annual shipments forecasts derived in the shipments analysis for the period 2014 (the base year) to 2050 (the end year of the analysis). The NIA shipments forecasts assume price elasticity of demand, whereby shipment volumes in the standards case decline relative to the base case as MPCs rise and, in doing so, drive up end-user purchase prices. See section IV.G. above and chapter 9 of the NOPR TSD for additional details.

Product and Capital Conversion Costs

An energy conservation standard would cause manufacturers to incur one-time conversion costs to bring their production facilities and product designs into compliance.

DOE evaluated the level of conversion-related expenditures that would be needed to comply with a design standard eliminating standing pilot lights. For the MIA, DOE classified these conversion costs into two major groups: (1) product conversion costs; and (2) capital conversion costs. Product conversion costs are one-time investments in research, development, testing, certification, marketing, and other non-capitalized costs necessary to make products comply with an energy conservation standard. Capital conversion costs are one-time investments in property, plant, and equipment necessary to adapt or change existing production facilities such that new compliant product designs can be fabricated and assembled.

To evaluate the level of capital conversion expenditures manufacturers would likely incur to comply with a potential energy conservation standard, DOE used manufacturer interviews to gather data on the anticipated level of capital investment that would be required to adapt to a design standard eliminating standing pilot lights. Based on manufacturer feedback, DOE estimated an average capital expenditure per manufacturer, which it then applied to the entire industry. DOE validated manufacturer comments through estimates of capital expenditure requirements derived from the product teardown analysis and engineering analysis described in chapter 5 of the NOPR TSD.

DOE assessed the product conversion costs by integrating quantitative and qualitative data. DOE considered feedback from manufacturers regarding potential product conversion costs and validated those numbers against engineering estimates of redesign efforts. Manufacturer data were aggregated to better reflect the industry as a whole and to protect confidential information.

DOE assumes that all conversion-related investments occur between the year of publication of the final rule and the year by which manufacturers must comply with the new standard. The conversion cost figures used in the GRIM can be found in section V.B.2 of this notice. For additional information on the estimated product and capital conversion costs, see chapter 12 of the NOPR TSD.

b. Government Regulatory Impact Model Scenarios

Markup Scenarios

Manufacturer selling prices (MSPs) include direct manufacturing production costs (i.e., labor, materials, and overhead estimated in DOE's MPCs) and all non-production costs (i.e., SG&A, R&D, and interest), along with profit. To calculate the MSPs in the GRIM, DOE applied non-production cost markups to the MPCs estimated in the engineering analysis. Modifying these markups in the standards case yields different sets of impacts on manufacturers. For the MIA, DOE modeled two standards-case markup scenarios to represent the uncertainty regarding the potential impacts on prices and profitability for manufacturers following the implementation of potential energy conservation standards: (1) a preservation of gross margin percentage markup scenario; and (2) a preservation of per-unit operating profit markup scenario. These scenarios lead to different markup values that, when applied to the inputted MPCs, result in varying revenue and cash flow impacts.

Under the preservation of gross margin percentage scenario, DOE applied a single uniform "gross margin percentage" markup across all efficiency levels, which assumes that manufacturers would be able to maintain the same amount of profit as a percentage of revenues at all efficiency levels for the product in question. As production costs increase with efficiency, this scenario implies that the absolute dollar markup will increase as well. Based on publicly-available financial information for manufacturers of gas hearth products, as well as comments received during manufacturer interviews, DOE assumed the average non-production cost markup—which includes SG&A expenses, R&D expenses, interest, and profit—to be 1.45 for all gas hearth products.

Because this markup scenario assumes that manufacturers would be able to maintain their gross margin percentage markups as production costs increase in response to an energy conservation standard, it represents a high bound to industry profitability, as manufacturers are able to fully pass through additional costs due to standards to consumers.

In the preservation of per unit operating profit scenario, manufacturer markups are set so that operating profit one year after the compliance date of the energy conservation standard is the same as in the base case on a per-unit basis. Under this scenario, as the costs of production increase under a standards case, manufacturers are generally required to reduce their markups to a level that maintains base-case operating profit per unit. The implicit assumption behind this markup scenario is that the industry can only maintain its operating profit in absolute dollars per unit after compliance with the new standard is required. Therefore, operating margin in percentage terms is reduced between the base case and standards case. DOE adjusted the manufacturer markups in the GRIM at each TSL to yield approximately the same earnings before interest and taxes in the standards case as in the base case. This markup scenario represents a low bound to industry profitability under an energy conservation standard, because manufacturers are not able to fully pass through to consumers the additional costs due to standards.

c. Manufacturer Interviews

As part of MIA, DOE discussed the potential impacts of an energy conservation standard with manufacturers of gas hearth products. The information gathered during these interviews enabled DOE to tailor the GRIM to reflect the unique financial characteristics of the industry. All interviews provided information that DOE used to evaluate the impacts of potential energy conservation standards on manufacturer cash flows, manufacturing capacities, and employment levels.

In interviews, DOE asked manufacturers to describe their concerns with the rulemaking regarding gas hearth products. The following section highlights manufacturer concerns that helped to shape DOE's understanding of potential impacts of an energy conservation standard on the industry. Manufacturer interviews are conducted under non-disclosure agreements (NDAs), so DOE does not document these discussions in the same way that it does public comments in the comment summaries. The following sections highlight the most significant of manufacturers' statements, although all concerns expressed by manufacturers were considered in DOE's analysis.

Impacts on Profitability

According to manufacturers, units with electronic ignition systems are more expensive to manufacture than units with standing pilot lights. Manufacturers indicated that purchasing components for electronic ignition systems increases per-unit production costs and, by extension, raises the retail price of products. Manufacturers stated that by driving up their cost of goods sold as well as the end-user purchase price, a standard eliminating standing pilot lights could lead to a drop in consumer demand. Because gas hearth products are not typically purchased exclusively for heating purposes but rather are valued by customers for their aesthetic appeal, manufacturers indicated that higher prices could depress demand if customers decide the decorative benefit of gas hearth products does not merit the higher costs. A fall in sales could, in turn, impact industry profitability.

Additionally, manufacturers stated that shipments of gas hearth products declined significantly over the last decade, in part due to the economic recession and a related decline in new-home construction. Several manufacturers forecast steady or declining shipments in future years absent an energy conservation standard. Those interviewed generally argued that if an energy conservation standard raises the price of gas hearth products, depresses demand, and reduces profitability, it could drive manufacturers to exit the market.

Impacts on Industry Competition

Small manufacturers expressed concern that an energy conservation standard for gas hearth products could alter the competitive dynamics of the market, favoring a subset of large manufacturers over their small-business competitors. Based on economies of scale, manufacturers that produce gas hearth products at high volumes are typically able to source components at lower per-unit prices than manufacturers that produce at lower volumes. In general, manufacturers of gas hearth products do not manufacture the components used for electronic ignition systems in-house. Rather, they source them from component suppliers. In interviews, manufacturers indicated that large manufacturers with high production volumes are able to source these components at relatively low cost. Small manufacturers with lower production volumes, in contrast, noted that the comparatively high cost they would incur to purchase electronic ignition system components would exacerbate the pricing advantage of large manufacturers and could lead to loss of price competitiveness for smaller players in the market.

Impacts on Product Performance

Multiple manufacturers stated that electronic ignition systems represent a more complicated and less reliable technology than standing pilot lights. These manufacturers indicated that units with electronic ignition systems often require more effort to repair and maintain. One manufacturer stated that electronic ignition systems account for a small fraction of their sales but the vast majority of their service calls, and several manufacturers suggested higher costs of maintaining units with electronic ignition systems compared to standing pilot lights. Additionally, several manufacturers suggested that electronic ignition systems are not as well suited to cold climates, where standing pilot lights may help to maintain buoyancy through the flue and to prevent condensation from building up on glass.

K. Emissions Analysis

In the emissions analysis, DOE estimated the reduction in emissions of carbon dioxide (CO_2), nitrogen oxides (NO_X), sulfur dioxide (SO_2), and mercury (Hg) from potential amended energy conservation standards for hearth products. In addition, DOE estimated emissions impacts in production activities (extracting, processing, and transporting fuels). These are referred to as "upstream" emissions. Together, these emissions account for the FFC. In accordance with DOE's FFC Statement of Policy (76 FR 51281 (Aug. 18, 2011) as amended at 77 FR 49701 (August 17, 2012)), the FFC analysis also includes impacts on emissions of methane (CH_4) and nitrous oxide (N_2O), both of which are recognized as greenhouse gases. The combustion emissions factors and the method DOE used to derive upstream emissions factors are described in chapter 13 of the NOPR TSD. The cumulative emissions reduction estimated for hearth products is presented in section V.B.6.

Today's proposed standard would reduce use of fuel at the site and slightly increase electricity use. DOE accounted for the associated reduction in site emissions and the upstream emissions associated with natural gas use, which include fugitive emissions. DOE also estimated the change in power sector emissions and the upstream emissions associated with electricity generation.

DOE primarily conducted the emissions analysis using emissions factors for CO_2 and most of the other gases derived from data in AEO 2014. Combustion emissions of CH_4 and N_2O were estimated using emissions intensity factors published by the U.S. Environmental Protection Agency (EPA) in its GHG Emissions Factors Hub.[53] Site emissions of CO_2 and NO_X were estimated using emissions intensity factors from a separate EPA publication.[54] DOE developed separate emissions factors for site, power sector, and upstream emissions. The method that DOE used to derive emissions factors is described in chapter 13 of the NOPR TSD.

For CH_4 and N_2O, DOE calculated emissions reduction in tons and also in terms of units of carbon dioxide equivalent (CO_2eq). Gases are converted to CO_2eq by multiplying each ton of the greenhouse gas by the gas's global warming potential (GWP) over a 100-year time horizon. Based on the Fifth Assessment Report of the Intergovernmental Panel on Climate Change,[55] DOE used GWP values of 28 for CH_4 and 265 for N_2O.

EIA prepares the AEO using the NEMS. Each annual version of NEMS incorporates the projected impacts of existing air quality regulations on emissions. AEO 2014 generally represents current legislation and environmental regulations, including

---

[53] See http://www.epa.gov/climateleadership/guidance/ghg-emissions.html.
[54] U.S. Environmental Protection Agency, Compilation of Air Pollutant Emission Factors, AP-42, Fifth Edition, Volume I: Stationary Point and Area Sources (1998) (Available at: http://www.epa.gov/ttn/chief/ap42/index.html).
[55] IPCC, 2013: Climate Change 2013: The Physical Science Basis. Contribution of Working Group I to the Fifth Assessment Report of the Intergovernmental Panel on Climate Change [Stocker, T.F., D. Qin, G.-K. Plattner, M. Tignor, S.K. Allen, J. Boschung, A. Nauels, Y. Xia, V. Bex and P.M. Midgley (eds.)]. Cambridge University Press, Cambridge, United Kingdom and New York, NY, USA. Chapter 8.

recent government actions, for which implementing regulations were available as of October 31, 2013.

Because the on-site operation of gas hearth products requires use of fossil fuels and results in emissions of CO_2, NO_X, and SO_2 at the sites where these appliances are used, DOE also accounted for the reduction in these site emissions and the associated upstream emissions due to potential standards.

SO_2 emissions from affected electric generating units (EGUs) are subject to nationwide and regional emissions cap-and-trade programs. Title IV of the Clean Air Act sets an annual emissions cap on SO_2 for affected EGUs in the 48 contiguous States and the District of Columbia (D.C.). (42 U.S.C. 7651 et seq.) SO_2 emissions from 28 eastern States and D.C. were also limited under the Clean Air Interstate Rule (CAIR; 70 FR 25162 (May 12, 2005)), which created an allowance-based trading program that operates along with the Title IV program. CAIR was remanded to the EPA by the U.S. Court of Appeals for the District of Columbia Circuit, but it remained in effect.[56] In 2011, EPA issued a replacement for CAIR, the Cross-State Air Pollution Rule (CSAPR). 76 FR 48208 (August 8, 2011). On August 21, 2012, the D.C. Circuit issued a decision to vacate CSAPR.[57] The court ordered EPA to continue administering CAIR. The

---

[56] See North Carolina v. EPA, 550 F.3d 1176 (D.C. Cir. 2008); North Carolina v. EPA, 531 F.3d 896 (D.C. Cir. 2008).
[57] See EME Homer City Generation, LP v. EPA, 696 F.3d 7, 38 (D.C. Cir. 2012), cert. granted, 81 U.S.L.W. 3567, 81 U.S.L.W. 3696, 81 U.S.L.W. 3702 (U.S. June 24, 2013) (No. 12-1182).

emissions factors used for today's NOPR, which are based on AEO 2014, assume that CAIR remains a binding regulation through 2040. [58]

The attainment of emissions caps is typically flexible among EGUs and is enforced through the use of emissions allowances and tradable permits. Beginning in 2016, however, SO_2 emissions will decline significantly as a result of the Mercury and Air Toxics Standards (MATS) for power plants. 77 FR 9304 (Feb. 16, 2012). In the final MATS rule, EPA established a standard for hydrogen chloride as a surrogate for acid gas hazardous air pollutants (HAP), and also established a standard for SO_2 (a non-HAP acid gas) as an alternative equivalent surrogate standard for acid gas HAP. The same controls are used to reduce HAP and non-HAP acid gas; thus, SO_2 emissions will be reduced as a result of the control technologies installed on coal-fired power plants to comply with the MATS requirements for acid gas. AEO 2014 assumes that, in order to continue operating, coal plants must have either flue gas desulfurization or dry sorbent injection systems installed by 2016. Both technologies, which are used to reduce acid gas emissions, also reduce SO_2 emissions. Under the MATS, emissions will be far below the cap established by CAIR, so it is likely that the increase in electricity demand associated with the highest hearth product efficiency levels would increase SO_2 emissions.

---

[58] On April 29, 2014, the U.S. Supreme Court reversed the judgment of the D.C. Circuit and remanded the case for further proceedings consistent with the Supreme Court's opinion. The Supreme Court held in part that EPA's methodology for quantifying emissions that must be eliminated in certain States due to their impacts in other downwind States was based on a permissible, workable, and equitable interpretation of the Clean Air Act provision that provides statutory authority for CSAPR. See EPA v. EME Homer City Generation, No 12-1182, slip op. at 32 (U.S. April 29, 2014). Because DOE is using emissions factors based on AEO 2014 for today's NOPR, the NOPR assumes that CAIR, not CSAPR, is the regulation in force. The difference between CAIR and CSAPR is not relevant for the purpose of DOE's analysis of SO_2 emissions.

CAIR established a cap on NO_X emissions in 28 eastern States and the District of Columbia.[59] Thus, it is unlikely that the increase in electricity demand associated with the considered hearth product standard would increase NO_X emissions in those States covered by CAIR. However, it would be expected to slightly increase power sector NO_X emissions in the States not affected by the caps, so DOE estimated NO_X emissions increases for these States. As shown in section V.B.6, however, the decrease in site NO_X emissions is much larger than the slight increase in power sector NO_X emissions.

The MATS limit mercury emissions from power plants, but they do not include emissions caps and, as such, the increase in electricity demand associated with the considered hearth product standard would be expected to slightly increase Hg emissions. DOE estimated mercury emissions using emissions factors based on AEO 2014, which incorporates the MATS.

L. Monetizing Carbon Dioxide and Other Emissions Impacts

As part of the development of this proposed rule, DOE considered the estimated monetary benefits from the reduced emissions of CO_2 and NO_X that are expected to result from the TSL considered. In order to make this calculation similar to the calculation of the NPV of consumer benefit, DOE considered the reduced emissions expected to result over the lifetime of equipment shipped in the forecast period. This section summarizes

---

[59] CSAPR also applies to NO_X, and it would supersede the regulation of NO_X under CAIR. As stated previously, the current analysis assumes that CAIR, not CSAPR, is the regulation in force. The difference between CAIR and CSAPR with regard to DOE's analysis of NO_X is slight.

the basis for the monetary values used for each of these emissions and presents the values considered in this rulemaking.

For today's NOPR, DOE is relying on a set of values for the social cost of carbon (SCC) that was developed by a Federal interagency process. A summary of the basis for these values is provided below, and a more detailed description of the methodologies used is provided as an appendix to chapter 14 of the NOPR TSD.

1. Social Cost of Carbon

The SCC is an estimate of the monetized damages associated with an incremental increase in carbon emissions in a given year. It is intended to include (but is not limited to) changes in net agricultural productivity, human health, property damages from increased flood risk, and the value of ecosystem services. Estimates of the SCC are provided in dollars per metric ton of carbon dioxide. A domestic SCC value is meant to reflect the value of damages in the United States resulting from a unit change in carbon dioxide emissions, while a global SCC value is meant to reflect the value of damages worldwide.

Under section 1(b)(6) of Executive Order 12866, "Regulatory Planning and Review," 58 FR 51735 (Oct. 4, 1993), agencies must, to the extent permitted by law, "assess both the costs and the benefits of the intended regulation and, recognizing that some costs and benefits are difficult to quantify, propose or adopt a regulation only upon a reasoned determination that the benefits of the intended regulation justify its costs."

The purpose of the SCC estimates presented here is to allow agencies to incorporate the monetized social benefits of reducing CO_2 emissions into cost-benefit analyses of regulatory actions. The estimates are presented with an acknowledgement of the many uncertainties involved and with a clear understanding that they should be updated over time to reflect increasing knowledge of the science and economics of climate impacts.

As part of the interagency process that developed the SCC estimates, technical experts from numerous agencies met on a regular basis to consider public comments, explore the technical literature in relevant fields, and discuss key model inputs and assumptions. The main objective of this process was to develop a range of SCC values using a defensible set of input assumptions grounded in the existing scientific and economic literatures. In this way, key uncertainties and model differences transparently and consistently inform the range of SCC estimates used in the rulemaking process.

a. Monetizing Carbon Dioxide Emissions

When attempting to assess the incremental economic impacts of carbon dioxide emissions, the analyst faces a number of challenges. A recent report from the National Research Council[60] points out that any assessment will suffer from uncertainty, speculation, and lack of information about: (1) future emissions of greenhouse gases; (2) the effects of past and future emissions on the climate system; (3) the impact of changes in climate on the physical and biological environment; and (4) the translation of these environmental impacts into economic damages. As a result, any effort to quantify and

_____

[60] National Research Council, Hidden Costs of Energy: Unpriced Consequences of Energy Production and Use, National Academies Press: Washington, DC (2009).

118

monetize the harms associated with climate change will raise questions of science, economics, and ethics and should be viewed as provisional.

Despite the limits of both quantification and monetization, SCC estimates can be useful in estimating the social benefits of reducing carbon dioxide emissions. The agency can estimate the benefits from reduced (or costs from increased) emissions in any future year by multiplying the change in emissions in that year by the SCC value appropriate for that year. The net present value of the benefits can then be calculated by multiplying each of these future benefits by an appropriate discount factor and summing across all affected years.

It is important to emphasize that the interagency process is committed to updating these estimates as the science and economic understanding of climate change and its impacts on society improves over time. In the meantime, the interagency group will continue to explore the issues raised by this analysis and consider public comments as part of the ongoing interagency process.

b. Development of Social Cost of Carbon Values

In 2009, an interagency process was initiated to offer a preliminary assessment of how best to quantify the benefits from reducing carbon dioxide emissions. To ensure consistency in how benefits are evaluated across agencies, the Administration sought to develop a transparent and defensible method, specifically designed for the rulemaking process, to quantify avoided climate change damages from reduced CO_2 emissions. The interagency group did not undertake any original analysis. Instead, it combined SCC estimates from the existing literature to use as interim values until a more comprehensive analysis could be conducted. The outcome of the preliminary assessment by the interagency group was a set of five interim values: global SCC estimates for 2007 (in 2006$) of $55, $33, $19, $10, and $5 per metric ton of CO_2. These interim values represented the first sustained interagency effort within the U.S. government to develop an SCC for use in regulatory analysis. The results of this preliminary effort were presented in several proposed and final rules.

c. Current Approach and Key Assumptions

After the release of the interim values, the interagency group reconvened on a regular basis to generate improved SCC estimates. Specifically, the group considered public comments and further explored the technical literature in relevant fields. The interagency group relied on three integrated assessment models commonly used to estimate the SCC: the FUND, DICE, and PAGE models. These models are frequently cited in the peer-reviewed literature and were used in the last assessment of the Intergovernmental Panel on Climate Change (IPCC). Each model was given equal weight in the SCC values that were developed.

Each model takes a slightly different approach to model how changes in emissions result in changes in economic damages. A key objective of the interagency process was to enable a consistent exploration of the three models, while respecting the different approaches to quantifying damages taken by the key modelers in the field. An extensive review of the literature was conducted to select three sets of input parameters

for these models: climate sensitivity, socio-economic and emissions trajectories, and

discount rates. A probability distribution for climate sensitivity was specified as an input

into all three models. In addition, the interagency group used a range of scenarios for the

socio-economic parameters and a range of values for the discount rate. All other model

features were left unchanged, relying on the model developers' best estimates and

judgments.

In 2010, the interagency group selected four sets of SCC values for use in

regulatory analyses. Three sets of values are based on the average SCC from three

integrated assessment models, at discount rates of 2.5 percent, 3 percent, and 5 percent.

The fourth set, which represents the 95th-percentile SCC estimate across all three models

at a 3-percent discount rate, is included to represent higher-than-expected impacts from

climate change further out in the tails of the SCC distribution. The values grow in real

terms over time. Additionally, the interagency group determined that a range of values

from 7 percent to 23 percent should be used to adjust the global SCC to calculate

domestic effects, although preference is given to consideration of the global benefits of

reducing CO_2 emissions.[61] Table IV.5 presents the values in the 2010 interagency group

report,[62] which is reproduced in appendix 14-A of the NOPR TSD.

---

[61] It is recognized that this calculation for domestic values is approximate, provisional, and highly speculative. There is no a priori reason why domestic benefits should be a constant fraction of net global damages over time.

[62] Social Cost of Carbon for Regulatory Impact Analysis Under Executive Order 12866, Interagency Working Group on Social Cost of Carbon, United States Government (February 2010) (Available at: http://www.whitehouse.gov/sites/default/files/omb/inforeg/for-agencies/Social-Cost-of-Carbon-for-RIA.pdf).

Table IV.5 Annual SCC Values from 2010 Interagency Report, 2010–2050 (in 2007 dollars per metric ton CO_2)

Year	Discount Rate			
	5%	3%	2.5%	3%
	Average	Average	Average	95th Percentile
2010	4.7	21.4	35.1	64.9
2015	5.7	23.8	38.4	72.8
2020	6.8	26.3	41.7	80.7
2025	8.2	29.6	45.9	90.4
2030	9.7	32.8	50.0	100.0
2035	11.2	36.0	54.2	109.7
2040	12.7	39.2	58.4	119.3
2045	14.2	42.1	61.7	127.8
2049	15.7	44.9	65.0	136.2

The SCC values used for today's notice were generated using the most recent versions of the three integrated assessment models that have been published in the peer-reviewed literature. Table IV.6 shows the updated sets of SCC estimates from the 2013 interagency update[63] in five-year increments from 2010 to 2050. Appendix 14-B of the NOPR TSD provides the full set of values. The central value that emerges is the average SCC across models at a 3-percent discount rate. However, for purposes of capturing the uncertainties involved in regulatory impact analysis, the interagency group emphasizes the importance of including all four sets of SCC values.

Table IV.6 Annual SCC Values from 2013 Interagency Update, 2010–2050 (in 2007 dollars per metric ton CO_2)

---

[63] Technical Update of the Social Cost of Carbon for Regulatory Impact Analysis Under Executive Order 12866, Interagency Working Group on Social Cost of Carbon, United States Government (May 2013; revised November 2013) (Available at: http://www.whitehouse.gov/sites/default/files/omb/assets/inforeg/technical-update-social-cost-of-carbon-for-regulator-impact-analysis.pdf).

Year	Discount Rate			
	5%	3%	2.5%	3%
	Average	Average	Average	95th Percentile
2010	11	32	51	89
2015	11	37	57	109
2020	12	43	64	128
2025	14	47	69	143
2030	16	52	75	159
2035	19	56	80	175
2040	21	61	86	191
2045	24	66	92	206
2049	26	71	97	220

It is important to recognize that a number of key uncertainties remain, and that current SCC estimates should be treated as provisional and revisable since they will evolve with improved scientific and economic understanding. The interagency group also recognizes that the existing models are imperfect and incomplete. The National Research Council report mentioned previously points out that there is tension between the goal of producing quantified estimates of the economic damages from an incremental ton of carbon and the limits of existing efforts to model these effects. There are a number of analytical challenges that are being addressed by the research community, including research programs housed in many of the Federal agencies participating in the interagency process to estimate the SCC. The interagency group intends to periodically review and reconsider those estimates to reflect increasing knowledge of the science and economics of climate impacts, as well as improvements in modeling.

In summary, in considering the potential global benefits resulting from reduced CO_2 emissions, DOE used the values from the 2013 interagency report, adjusted to 2013$

using the Gross Domestic Product price deflator. For each of the four SCC cases specified, the values used for emissions in 2015 were $12.0, $40.5, $62.4, and $119 per metric ton avoided (values expressed in 2013$). DOE derived values after 2050 using the relevant growth rates for the 2040-2050 period in the interagency update.

DOE multiplied the CO_2 emissions reduction estimated for each year by the SCC value for that year in each of the four cases. To calculate a present value of the stream of monetary values, DOE discounted the values in each of the four cases using the specific discount rate that had been used to obtain the SCC values in each case.

2. Valuation of Other Emissions Reductions

As noted previously, DOE has taken into account how the considered energy conservation standard would reduce site NO_X emissions nationwide and increase power sector NO_X emissions in those 22 States not affected by the CAIR. DOE estimated the monetized value of net NO_X emissions reductions based on estimates found in the relevant scientific literature. Estimates of monetary value for reducing NO_X from stationary sources range from $476 to $4,893 per ton in 2013$.[64] DOE calculated monetary benefits using a medium value for NO_X emissions of $2,684 per short ton (in 2013$) and real discount rates of 3 percent and 7 percent.

---

[64] U.S. Office of Management and Budget, Office of Information and Regulatory Affairs, 2006 Report to Congress on the Costs and Benefits of Federal Regulations and Unfunded Mandates on State, Local, and Tribal Entities (2006) (Available at: http://www.whitehouse.gov/sites/default/files/omb/assets/omb/inforeg/2006_cb/2006_cb_final_report.pdf).

DOE is evaluating appropriate monetization of avoided SO_2 and Hg emissions in energy conservation standards rulemakings. DOE has not included monetization of those emissions in the current analysis.

M. Utility Impact Analysis

The utility impact analysis estimates several effects on the power generation industry that would result from the adoption of new or amended energy conservation standards. In the utility impact analysis, DOE analyzes the changes in installed electrical capacity and generation that would result for each trial standard level. The analysis is based on published output from NEMS, which is a public domain, multi-sectored, partial equilibrium model of the U.S. energy sector. Each year, NEMS is updated to produce the AEO reference case, as well as a number of side cases that estimate the economy-wide impacts of changes to energy supply and demand. DOE uses those published side cases that incorporate efficiency-related policies to estimate the marginal impacts of reduced energy demand on the utility sector. The output of this analysis is a set of time-dependent coefficients that capture the change in electricity generation, primary fuel consumption, installed capacity and power sector emissions due to a unit reduction in demand for a given end use. These coefficients are multiplied by the stream of electricity savings calculated in the NIA to provide estimates of selected utility impacts of new or amended energy conservation standards. Chapter 15 of the NOPR TSD describes the utility impact analysis in further detail.

N. Employment Impact Analysis

Employment impacts from new or amended energy conservation standards include direct and indirect impacts. Direct employment impacts are any changes in the number of employees of manufacturers of the products subject to standards; the MIA addresses those impacts. Indirect employment impacts are changes in national employment that occur due to the shift in expenditures and capital investment caused by the purchase and operation of more-efficient appliances. Indirect employment impacts from standards consist of the jobs created or eliminated in the national economy, other than in the manufacturing sector being regulated, due to: (1) reduced spending by end users on energy; (2) reduced spending on new energy supply by the utility industry; (3) increased consumer spending on the purchase of new products; and (4) the effects of those three factors throughout the economy.

One method for assessing the possible effects on the demand for labor of such shifts in economic activity is to compare sector employment statistics developed by the Labor Department's Bureau of Labor Statistics (BLS). BLS regularly publishes its estimates of the number of jobs per million dollars of economic activity in different sectors of the economy, as well as the jobs created elsewhere in the economy by this same economic activity. Data from BLS indicate that expenditures in the utility sector generally create fewer jobs (both directly and indirectly) than expenditures in other sectors of the economy.[65] There are many reasons for these differences, including wage differences and the fact that the utility sector is more capital-intensive and less labor-

---

[65] See Bureau of Economic Analysis, "Regional Multipliers: A Handbook for the Regional Input-Output Modeling System (RIMS II)," U.S. Department of Commerce (1992).

intensive than other sectors. Energy conservation standards have the effect of reducing consumer utility bills. Because reduced consumer expenditures for energy likely lead to increased expenditures in other sectors of the economy, the general effect of efficiency standards is to shift economic activity from a less labor-intensive sector (i.e., the utility sector) to more labor-intensive sectors (e.g., the retail and service sectors). Thus, based on the BLS data alone, DOE believes net national employment may increase because of shifts in economic activity resulting from standards for hearth products.

For the standard considered in this NOPR, DOE estimated indirect national employment impacts using an input/output model of the U.S. economy called Impact of Sector Energy Technologies, Version 3.1.1 (ImSET).[66] ImSET is a special-purpose version of the "U.S. Benchmark National Input-Output" (I–O) model, which was designed to estimate the national employment and income effects of energy-saving technologies. The ImSET software includes a computer-based I–O model having structural coefficients that characterize economic flows among the 187 sectors. ImSET's national economic I–O structure is based on a 2002 U.S. benchmark table, specially aggregated to the 187 sectors most relevant to industrial, commercial, and residential building energy use. DOE notes that ImSET is not a general equilibrium forecasting model and understands the uncertainties involved in projecting employment impacts, especially changes in the later years of the analysis. Because ImSET does not incorporate price changes, the employment effects predicted by ImSET may over-

---

[66] M.J. Scott, O.V. Livingston, P.J. Balducci, J.M. Roop, and R.W. Schultz, ImSET 3.1: Impact of Sector Energy Technologies, PNNL-18412, Pacific Northwest National Laboratory (2009) (Available at: www.pnl.gov/main/publications/external/technical_reports/PNNL-18412.pdf).

estimate actual job impacts over the long run. For the NOPR, DOE used ImSET only to estimate short-term (through 2026) employment impacts.

For more details on the employment impact analysis, see chapter 16 of the NOPR TSD.

V. Analytical Results and Conclusions

The following section addresses the results from DOE's analyses with respect to a potential energy conservation standard for hearth products. Additional details regarding the analyses conducted by DOE are contained in the publicly-available NOPR TSD supporting this notice.

A. Trial Standard Levels

DOE typically considers multiple TSLs for a standards rulemaking. However, the hearth products rulemaking is proposing a prescriptive standard that would disallow the use of continuously-burning pilots, thereby largely eliminating the standby mode energy consumption of these products. The analysis is considering an established alternative to a standing pilot, which is an intermittent pilot. Other options that are present in other combustion appliances, such as hot surface ignition, are virtually non-existent in the hearth product market primarily due to the increased cost and additional engineering challenges. Therefore, hearth products have only one TSL, which reflects a standard that would disallow the use of a standing pilot. For the purposes of this analysis, TSL1 assumes that all covered hearth products would use an intermittent pilot (see Table V.1).

Table V.1 Trial Standard Level for Hearth Products

Ignition Type	TSL 1
Standing Pilot	0%
Intermittent Pilot	100%

B. Economic Justification and Energy Savings

1. Economic Impacts on Individual Consumers

DOE analyzed the economic impacts of the proposed rule on hearth products

consumers by looking at the effect on the LCC and the PBP. DOE also examined the

impacts of potential standards on consumer subgroups. These analyses are discussed

below.

a. Life-Cycle Cost and Payback Period

In general, higher-efficiency products affect consumers in two ways: (1) purchase

price typically increases, and (2) annual operating costs typically decrease. Inputs used

for calculating the LCC and PBP include total installed costs (i.e., product price plus

installation costs), and operating costs (i.e., annual energy savings, energy prices, energy

price trends, repair costs, and maintenance costs). The LCC calculation also uses product

lifetime and a discount rate.

Table V.2 shows the LCC and PBP results for the considered TSL. The simple

payback is measured relative to the baseline product, and reflects the number of years it

would take for the consumer to recover the increased costs of higher-efficiency products as a result of operating cost savings. The PBP is an economic benefit-cost measure that uses benefits and costs without discounting. Table V.3 shows the LCC savings relative to the base case in the compliance year. Additionally, 23 percent of consumers experience net cost because their standing pilot lights have relatively low hours of operation, and thus achieve modest energy savings from using an intermittent pilot ignition.

Table V.2 Average LCC and PBP Results by Efficiency Level for Hearth Products

| TSL | Design | Average Costs 2013$ | | | | Simple Payback years | Average Lifetime years |
		Installed Cost	First Year's Operating Cost	Lifetime Operating Cost	LCC		
1	Intermittent Pilot	$268	$15	$174	$442	2.9	15.0

Note: The results are calculated assuming that all consumers use products with that design. The simple PBP is measured relative to the baseline product.

Table V.3 LCC Savings Relative to the Base-Case Efficiency Distribution for Hearth Products

| TSL | Design | Life-Cycle Cost Savings | |
		% of Consumers that Experience Net Cost	Average Savings* 2013$
1	Intermittent Pilot	23%	$165

* The calculation includes households with zero LCC savings (no impact).

b. Consumer Subgroup Analysis

In the consumer subgroup analysis, DOE estimated the impacts of the considered standard on senior-only households. The average LCC savings and simple PBPs for senior-only households are shown in Table V.4. The LCC savings are somewhat lower for the senior-only subgroup. Chapter 11 of the NOPR TSD presents detailed results of the consumer subgroup analysis.

Table V.4. Comparison of Impacts for Consumer Subgroups with All Consumers, Hearth Products

TSL	Average LCC Savings 2013$		Simple Payback Period Years	
	Senior-Only	All Consumers	Senior-Only	All Consumers
1	$121	$165	3.5	2.9

c. Rebuttable Presumption Payback Period

As discussed in section III.G.2, EPCA establishes a rebuttable presumption that an energy conservation standard is economically justified if the increased purchase cost for a product that meets the standard is less than three times the value of the first-year energy savings resulting from the standard. Accordingly, DOE calculated a rebuttable-presumption PBP for the proposed hearth products standard based on the average energy use and costs calculated in the LCC analysis. DOE routinely conducts an economic analysis that considers the full range of impacts to the consumer, manufacturer, Nation, and environment, as required by EPCA under 42 U.S.C. 6295(o)(2)(B)(i). The results of that analysis serve as the basis for DOE to definitively evaluate the economic justification for a potential standard level, thereby supporting or rebutting the results of any preliminary determination of economic justification. Table V.5 shows the rebuttable-presumption PBP for the considered TSL for hearth products.

Table V.5. Rebuttable-Presumption Payback Periods (years) for Hearth Products

Product	Rebuttable Presumption Payback (years)
	TSL 1
Hearth Products	2.3

2. Economic Impacts on Manufacturers

DOE performed a manufacturer impact analysis (MIA) to estimate the impact of an energy conservation standard on manufacturers of gas hearth products. The following section describes the expected impacts on manufacturers of a ban on standing pilot lights. Chapter 12 of the NOPR TSD explains the analysis in further detail.

a. Industry Cash Flow Analysis Results

Table V.6 and Table V.7depict a range of estimated financial impacts (represented by changes in industry net present value, or INPV) of an energy conservation standard on manufacturers of gas hearth products, as well as the conversion costs that DOE expects manufacturers would incur to comply with the standard.

As discussed in section IV.J.2, DOE modeled two different markup scenarios to evaluate the range of cash flow impacts on the gas hearth industry: (1) the preservation of gross margin percentage markup scenario; and (2) the preservation of per-unit operating profit markup scenario. Each of these scenarios is discussed immediately below.

To assess the less severe end of the range of potential impacts, DOE modeled a preservation of gross margin percentage markup scenario, in which a uniform "gross margin percentage" markup is applied. In this scenario, DOE assumed that a manufacturer's absolute dollar markup would increase as production costs increase in the standards case.

To assess the more severe end of the range of potential impacts, DOE modeled the preservation of per-unit operating profit markup scenario, which reflects manufacturer concerns surrounding their inability to maintain margins as manufacturing production costs increase to comply with an energy conservation standard. In this scenario, as manufacturers incur higher costs of goods sold and make the investments necessary to produce new standards-compliant products, their percentage markup decreases. Operating profit does not change in absolute dollars but decreases as a percentage of revenue.

As noted in the MIA methodology discussion (see section IV.J.2), in addition to markup scenarios, the MPC, shipments, and conversion cost assumptions also affect INPV results.

Each of the modeled scenarios results in a unique set of cash flows and corresponding industry values under an energy conservation standard. In the following discussion, the INPV results refer to the difference in industry value between the base case and the standards case that results from the sum of discounted cash flows from the base year 2014 through 2050, the end of the analysis period. To provide perspective on the short-run cash flow impact, DOE includes in the discussion of results a comparison of free cash flow between the base case and the standards case in the year before the standard would take effect. This figure provides an understanding of the magnitude of the required conversion costs relative to the cash flow generated by the industry in the base case.

Table V.6 presents estimated financial impacts under the preservation of gross margin percentage markup scenario, and Table V.7 presents impacts under the preservation of per-unit operating profit markup scenario. Estimated conversion costs and free cash flow in the year prior to the compliance date of the standard do not vary with markup scenario.

Table V.6. Manufacturer Impact Analysis Results Under the Preservation of Gross Margin Percentage Markup Scenario

	Units	Base Case	Standards Case*
INPV	2013$M	125.3	125.8
Change in INPV	2013$M	-	0.5
	%	-	0.4
Product Conversion Costs	2013$M	-	7.8
Capital Conversion Costs	2013$M	-	0.9
Total Conversion Costs	2013$M	-	8.7
Free Cash Flow (base case = 2020)	2013$M	10.9	8.2
Change in Free Cash Flow	2013$M	-	(2.6)
	%	-	(24.0)

*Parentheses indicate negative values

Table V.7 Manufacturer Impact Analysis Results Under the Preservation of Per-Unit Operating Profit Markup Scenario

	Units	Base Case	Standards Case*
INPV	2013$M	125.3	122.0
Change in INPV	2013$M	-	(3.3)
	%	-	(2.6)
Product Conversion Costs	2013$M	-	7.8
Capital Conversion Costs	2013$M	-	0.9
Total Conversion Costs	2013$M	-	8.7
Free Cash Flow (base case = 2020)	2013$M	10.9	8.2
Change in Free Cash Flow	2013$M	-	(2.6)
Flow	%	-	(24.0)

DOE estimates the impacts of an energy conservation standard on INPV to range from -$3.3 million to $0.5 million, or a change of -2.6 percent to 0.4 percent. Industry free cash flow is estimated to decrease by $2.6 million, or a change of -24.0 percent compared to the base-case value of $10.9 million in the year before the compliance date (2020).

The capital and product conversion costs required to bring non-compliant models into compliance with standards drive the lower-bound negative INPV results at this level. To bring all non-compliant products into compliance, DOE estimates total industry conversion costs of $8.7 million. This estimate assumes that all non-compliant models (i.e., models with standing pilot lights) would be redesigned to accommodate electronic ignition systems. This represents a conservative assumption, as manufacturers may choose to discontinue some models with standing pilot lights. Models already available with the option of electronic ignition would not require any one-time conversion costs by the manufacturer in order to achieve compliance.

During interviews, some manufacturers expressed concern that an energy conservation standard could pose a significant conversion cost burden with regard to labeling requirements. Under Canadian law, manufacturers must test and label gas fireplaces, stoves, and inserts with a fireplace efficiency (FE) rating. If a Federal energy conservation standard mandated an alternative efficiency metric for hearth products (e.g., AFUE), manufacturers indicated they could be required to hold separate SKUs for the Canadian and U.S. markets in order to comply with each jurisdiction's requirements.

However, because the proposed standard is a prescriptive design requirement and does not establish a minimum efficiency rating or require products to be labeled with a particular efficiency metric, DOE did not factor the cost of holding duplicate SKUs into its conversion cost model.

Beyond conversion costs, the change in MPCs also impact manufacturer financials. The cost to manufacturers of producing equipment with electronic ignition systems tends to be greater than the cost of producing equipment with standing pilot lights. A higher per-unit manufacturer production cost could, in turn, result in a higher per-unit retail price to the end user. In interviews, manufacturers expressed concerned that higher prices could lead to a change in industry shipments. The increase in MPC and the change in pricing to the manufacturer's first customer are reflected in the GRIM and in the INPV results. Shipments used in the GRIM are consistent with the Shipments Analysis, presented in section IV.G, which includes assumptions regarding price elasticity of demand.

DOE requests feedback on the expected total conversion costs for the industry. This is identified as Issue 20 in section VII.E, "Issues on Which DOE Seeks Comment."

b. Direct Impacts on Employment

To quantitatively assess the potential impacts of energy conservation standards on direct employment in the gas hearth industry, DOE used the GRIM to estimate the domestic labor expenditures and number of employees in the base case and the standards case from 2014 through 2050. DOE used statistical data from the U.S. Census Bureau's 2011 Annual Survey of Manufacturers,[67] the results of the engineering analysis, and interviews with manufacturers to determine the inputs necessary to calculate industry-wide labor expenditures and domestic direct employment levels. Labor expenditures related to manufacturing of the product are a function of the labor intensity of the product, the sales volume, and an assumption that wages remain fixed in real terms over time. The total labor expenditures in each year are calculated by multiplying the MPCs by the labor percentage of MPCs.

The total labor expenditures in the GRIM were then converted to domestic production employment levels by dividing production labor expenditures by the annual payment per production worker (production worker hours times the labor rate found in the U.S. Census Bureau's 2011 Annual Survey of Manufacturers). The production worker estimates in this section only cover workers up to the line-supervisor level who are directly involved in fabricating and assembling a product within an original equipment manufacturer (OEM) facility. Workers performing services that are closely associated with production operations, such as materials handling tasks using forklifts, are also included as production labor. DOE's estimates only account for production workers who manufacture the specific products covered by this rulemaking. The direct employment impacts calculated represent a range of potential changes in the number of production workers resulting from an energy conservation standard for hearth products, as compared to the base case.

---

[67] U.S. Census Bureau, Annual Survey of Manufacturers: General Statistics: Statistics for Industry Groups and Industries (2011) (Available at http://www.census.gov/manufacturing/asm/index.html).

To estimate an upper bound to employment change, DOE assumes all domestic manufacturers would continue producing the same scope of covered products in the U.S. and would not move production to foreign countries. To estimate a lower bound to employment, DOE assumes manufacturers would not redesign any non-compliant models and that there would be a proportionate loss of production employment.

Table V.8 Table V.8 shows the estimated range of impacts of a potential energy conservation standard on U.S. production workers of gas hearth products. In the base case, DOE estimates that the gas hearth industry would employ 1,565 domestic production workers in 2021, the first full year of compliance. DOE estimates that 86 percent of gas hearth products sold in the United States are manufactured domestically.

Table V.8 Potential Changes in the Total Number of Production Workers in the Gas Hearth Industry in 2021

	Base Case	Standards Case
Domestic Production Workers in 2021	1,565	657 to 1,514
Potential Changes in Domestic Production Workers in 2021*	-	(908) to (51)

* DOE presents a range of potential employment impacts. Parentheses indicate negative values.

The less severe end of the range of potential employment impacts estimates a loss of 51 domestic production jobs in 2021 in the standards case. This assumes manufacturers would continue to produce the same scope of covered products within the United States. However, because the shipment model predicts a decline in shipment volumes under an energy conservation standard, DOE estimates a related reduction in labor inputs and employment.

The more severe end of the range represents the maximum decrease in total number of U.S. production workers that could be expected to result from an energy conservation standard. For the hearths industry, DOE assumed a worst-case scenario in which all products sold with standing pilot lights in the base case would be eliminated in the standards case and would not be replaced by any additional sales of compliant products. DOE then assumed industry labor requirements would shrink in proportion to lost sales volumes The NIA shipments analysis forecasts that 58 percent of base-case shipments would consist of units with standing pilot lights in 2021. Based on the worst-case scenario assumptions above, DOE modeled a 58-percent decline in direct production employment. As a result, DOE estimates a loss of up to 908 domestic production jobs in 2021 resulting from a design standard that eliminates standing pilot lights.

This conclusion is independent of any conclusions regarding indirect employment impacts in the broader United States economy, which are documented in chapter 15 of the NOPR TSD.

DOE requests comment on the portion of the industry's hearths production consisting of units equipped with standing pilot lights and on potential direct employment impacts resulting from a requirement for the elimination of standing pilot lights. This is identified as Issue 21 in section VII.E, "Issues on Which DOE Seeks Comment."

c. Impacts on Manufacturing Capacity

According to gas hearth manufacturers interviewed, a requirement eliminating standing pilot lights would not likely constrain manufacturing production capacity. Converting a gas hearth product's ignition system from a standing pilot light to an electronic ignition system is primarily a matter of purchasing and assembling different ignition system components. While this may entail higher costs for purchased parts and changes in assembly, it is not likely to impede manufacturers' capacity to continue producing gas hearth equipment in line with demand. Moreover, several manufacturers stated that the higher costs of producing equipment with electronic ignition systems could lead to a decline in demand, potentially leaving them with excess production capacity. Accordingly, DOE does not believe manufacturers will face capacity constraints as a result of today's proposed standard.

d. Impacts on Subgroups of Manufacturers

As discussed above, using average cost assumptions to develop an industry cash flow estimate is not adequate for assessing differential impacts among subgroups of manufacturers. Small manufacturers, niche players, or manufacturers exhibiting a cost structure that differs largely from the industry average could be affected disproportionately. For the hearth products industry, DOE used the results of the industry characterization to group manufacturers exhibiting similar characteristics. Specifically,

DOE identified and separately evaluated the impacts of an energy conservation standard on two subgroups of manufacturers: (1) manufacturers of gas log sets and (2) small business manufacturers.

During interviews, multiple manufacturers commented that gas log sets represent a distinct market segment within the gas hearth industry. These manufacturers indicated that gas log sets serve a different market niche and face different space constraints than other gas hearth products. Additionally, gas log sets often sell at lower prices than other gas hearth products. As a result, an increase in manufacturing costs and, by extension, retail price resulting from an energy conservation standard could have a proportionally greater impact on gas log sets relative to other gas hearth products.

Gas log sets are typically designed for use in existing wood-burning fireplaces. During interviews, manufacturers of gas log sets stated that unlike other gas hearth products, gas log sets compete with wood, coal, and wood/wax logs. These alternatives are typically inexpensive to purchase, such that consumers could feasibly substitute away from gas log sets and toward wood and/or wood/wax logs if an energy conservation standard leads to higher prices. According to these manufacturers, if design constraints specific to gas log sets cause an energy conservation standard to alter product aesthetics, it could further drive consumer product-switching.

Because gas log sets are designed to fit within existing wood-burning fireplaces, manufacturers indicated that design options for gas log sets are constrained by the geometric configurations of pre-existing fireplaces. Manufacturers stated that electronic ignition systems take up more space than standing pilot lights and that accommodating electronic ignition systems inside existing fireplaces could, in turn, reduce the size of the gas log sets consumers could purchase for their fireplaces. Manufacturers also indicated that electronic ignition system components can be difficult to conceal within a gas log set's design. Unlike other gas hearth products, gas log sets are not sold as part of a packaged unit, leaving manufacturers with limited options for obscuring the gas valve, pilot assembly, control module, wiring, and other components that make up an electronic ignition system. As a result, these components may be more exposed when used with gas log sets compared to other gas hearth products. Manufacturers also stated that electric outlets may not be situated in close enough proximity to wood-burning fireplaces to enable ready installation of units with electronic ignition systems. In such cases, the need for extension cords could impact the aesthetic appeal of products. Alternatively, hiring an electrician could raise installation costs and potentially deter price-sensitive consumers.

Alongside aesthetic impacts, manufacturers expressed concern regarding the cost implications of a potential ban on standing pilot lights. As discussed previously, purchasing components for electronic ignition systems typically costs manufacturers more than purchasing components for standing pilot lights. Higher manufacturing costs, in turn, lead to higher retail prices. To estimate the potential difference in cost resulting from a requirement eliminating standing pilot lights, DOE modeled the manufacturer production costs (MPCs) for both vented and unvented gas log sets using both standing pilot lights and electronic ignition systems. DOE similarly modeled MPCs for other categories of gas hearth products. Table V.9presents the relative increase in MPC for products manufactured with electronic ignition systems as opposed to standing pilot lights. See chapter 5 of the TSD for a more detailed discussion of how MPCs were calculated.

Table V.9. Relative Cost Impacts of Converting Gas Log Sets from Standing Pilot Lights to Electronic Ignition Systems

Product Group	Estimated Increase in MPC of Switching from Standing Pilot to Electronic Ignition*	% Increase in MPC of Ignition System	% Increase in Overall MPC
Vented Fireplace/Insert/Stove	$28	56%	9%
Unvented Fireplace/Insert/Stove	$32	47%	11%
Vented Gas Logs	$70	227%	37%
Unvented Gas Logs	$56	194%	27%
Outdoor	$55	65%	26%

* DOE understands that standing pilot ignitions largely use two styles of gas valves: (1) manual and (2) millivolt. The incremental costs of switching from standing pilot lights to electronic ignition systems presented here assume gas fireplaces, inserts, and stoves use standing pilot lights with millivolt gas valves while gas log sets and outdoor hearth products use standing pilot lights with manual gas valves. The millivolt gas valve uses a thermopile placed in the pilot light to generate a voltage difference, thereby allowing a remote control to be used to turn the burner on and off. These valves are larger and more expensive than manual gas valves, which are operated by hand. Based on public comments on previous rulemakings and manufacturer interviews, DOE recognizes the importance of space constraints and cost burden associated with control systems for gas log sets. For the purposes of analysis, DOE chose to represent gas log sets with standing pilots using manual gas valves. Fireplaces, inserts, and stoves provide more opportunity to package and conceal larger, more complex ignition systems. Accordingly, DOE chose to represent the standing pilot variation of this product category with models using millivolt gas valves.

As the results above indicate, DOE estimates that the cost of switching from a standing pilot light to an electronic ignition system could disproportionately impact gas log set manufacturers. These results are driven by two primary factors. First, the results are based on the assumption that gas log sets use standing pilot lights with manual gas valves, which are smaller and less expensive than standing pilot lights with millivolt gas

143

valves. Under this assumption, the higher cost of purchasing electronic ignition system components would represent a more significant expenditure in absolute dollars for manufacturers of gas log sets using manual standing pilot lights relative to manufacturers of other hearth products (e.g. fireplaces, inserts, and stoves) using more expensive millivolt standing pilot lights. Second, the overall cost of manufacturing gas log sets is often lower than the overall cost of manufacturing other types of gas hearth products. This means the same increase in MPC in absolute dollars would result in a higher proportional increase in MPC for gas log sets. Assuming, as described above, that manufacturers of gas log sets are likely to see a greater increase in MPC in absolute dollars compared to manufacturers of other products, this would imply an even greater proportional increase in overall MPC of gas log sets. If retail prices scale with MPCs, manufacturers indicated that demand for gas log sets from price-sensitive consumers could decline and, in turn, negatively impact manufacturer profitability.

For the small business subgroup analysis, DOE applied the small business size standards published by the Small Business Administration (SBA) to determine whether a company is considered a small business. 65 FR 30836, 30848 (May 15, 2000), as amended at 65 FR 53533, 53544 (Sept. 5, 2000) and codified at 13 CFR part 121. To be categorized as a small business, a gas hearth product manufacturer and its affiliates may employ a maximum of 500 employees. This 500-employee threshold includes all employees in a business's parent company and any other subsidiaries and applies to all hearth products, categorized respectively under North American Industry Classification System (NAICS) code 333414, "Heating Equipment (Except Warm Air Furnaces)

Manufacturing" and NAICS code 335228, "Other Major Household Appliance Manufacturing." Based on this classification, DOE identified at least 66 manufacturers that qualify as domestic small businesses.

Small business concerns surrounding the proposed standard centered on issues of purchasing power and economies of scale. During interviews, small manufacturers expressed concern regarding the impact of eliminating standing pilot lights on their ability to compete with larger manufacturers. Because large manufacturers often produce at higher volumes, they may be able to source components for electronic ignition systems at lower per-unit prices than small manufacturers that produce at lower volumes. If the per-unit production costs increase more for small manufacturers than for large manufacturers, and if small manufacturers are not able to pass costs through to price-sensitive consumers, they could potentially face reduced markups and profits, as well as a decline in market share. The impacts on small business manufacturers are discussed in greater detail in the regulatory flexibility analysis, in section VI.B of this notice and in chapter 12 of the NOPR TSD.

e. Cumulative Regulatory Burden

While any one regulation may not impose a significant burden on manufacturers, the combined effects of several recent impending regulations may have serious consequences for some manufacturers, groups of manufacturers, or an entire industry. Assessing the impact of a single regulation may overlook this cumulative regulatory burden. Multiple regulations affecting the same manufacturer can strain profits and can

145

lead companies to abandon product lines or markets with lower expected future returns than competing products. For these reasons, DOE conducts an analysis of cumulative regulatory burden as part of its rulemakings pertaining to appliance efficiency.

For the cumulative regulatory burden analysis, DOE looks at other product-specific Federal regulations that could affect gas hearth product manufacturers and that will take effect approximately three years before or after the 2021 compliance date of the proposed energy conservation standard. In interviews, manufacturers cited a Consumer Product Safety Commission regulation requiring barrier screens on gas hearth products. However, this requirement is set to take effect in January 2015 and, therefore, is not considered in this analysis. DOE did not identify any other Federally-mandated product-specific regulations that will take effect in the three years before or after the 2021 compliance date for this rulemaking and, therefore, has not presented any other regulations in this analysis of cumulative regulatory burden.

DOE requests comment on product-specific regulations that take effect between 2018 and 2024 that would contribute to manufacturers' cumulative regulatory burden. DOE requests information identifying the specific regulations, as well as data quantifying the associated cost burden on manufacturers. This is identified as Issue 22 in section VII.E, "Issues on Which DOE Seeks Comment."

3. National Impact Analysis

The shipments projections are a key input to the NIA. The base case forecast shows shipments of the covered product growing from approximately 978,000 in 2021 to 980,000 in 2050.

a. Significance of Energy Savings

DOE projected energy savings for hearth products purchased in the 30-year period that begins in the first full year of anticipated compliance with the proposed standard (2021–2050). The savings are measured over the entire lifetime of products purchased in the 30-year period. DOE quantified the energy savings attributable to the considered TSL as the difference in energy consumption between the standards case and the base case. Table V.10 presents the estimated primary and FFC energy savings. The approach for estimating national energy savings is further described in section IV.H.1.

Table V.10 Cumulative National Primary and FFC Energy Savings for Hearth Products Sold in 2021–2050

Product	Energy Savings	Trial Standard Level
		(quads)
Hearth Products	Primary	0.62
	Full-Fuel-Cycle	0.69

OMB Circular A-4[68] requires agencies to present analytical results, including separate schedules of the monetized benefits and costs that show the type and timing of benefits and costs. Circular A-4 also directs agencies to consider the variability of key elements underlying the estimates of benefits and costs. For this rulemaking, DOE

---

[68] U.S. Office of Management and Budget, "Circular A-4: Regulatory Analysis" (Sept. 17, 2003) (Available at: http://www.whitehouse.gov/omb/circulars_a004_a-4/).

undertook a sensitivity analysis using 9, rather than 30, years of product shipments. The choice of a 9-year period is a proxy for the timeline in EPCA for the review of certain energy conservation standards and potential revision of and compliance with such revised standards.[69] The review timeframe established in EPCA is generally not synchronized with the product lifetime, product manufacturing cycles, or other factors specific to hearth products. Thus, such results are presented for informational purposes only and are not indicative of any change in DOE's analytical methodology. The impacts are counted over the lifetime of hearth products purchased in 2021–2029. Table V.11 shows the national FFC energy savings for this period.

Table V.11. Cumulative National FFC Energy Savings for the Trial Standard Level for Hearth Products Sold in 2021–2029

Product	Trial Standard Level
	(quads)
	1
Hearth Products	0.21

b. Net Present Value of Consumer Costs and Benefits

DOE estimated the cumulative NPV of the total costs and savings for consumers that would result from the TSL considered for hearth products. In accordance with

---

[69] Section 325(m) of EPCA requires DOE to review its standards at least once every 6 years, and requires, for certain products, a 3-year period after any new standard is promulgated before compliance is required, except that in no case may any new standards be required within 6 years of the compliance date of the previous standards. While adding a 6-year review to the 3-year compliance period adds up to 9 years, DOE notes that it may undertake reviews at any time within the 6 year period and that the 3-year compliance date may yield to the 6-year backstop. A 9-year analysis period may not be appropriate given the variability that occurs in the timing of standards reviews and the fact that for some consumer products, the compliance period is 5 years rather than 3 years.

OMB's guidelines on regulatory analysis,[70] DOE calculated the NPV using both a 7-percent and a 3-percent real discount rate. Table V.12 shows the consumer NPV results for the TSL considered for hearth products. In each case, the impacts cover the lifetime of products purchased in 2021–2050.

Table V.12. Cumulative Net Present Value of Consumer Benefits for the Trial Standard Level for Hearth Products Sold in 2021–2050

Product	Discount Rate (%)	Trial Standard Level
Product Class	Discount Rate %	Trial Standard Level
		(billion 2013$)
Hearth Products	3%	3.12
	7%	1.03

The NPV results based on the aforementioned nine-year analytical period are presented in Table V.13. The impacts are counted over the lifetime of products purchased in 2021–2029. As mentioned previously, such results are presented for informational purposes only and are not indicative of any change in DOE's analytical methodology or decision criteria.

Table V.13. Cumulative Net Present Value of Consumer Benefits for the Trial Standard Level for Hearth Products Sold in 2021–2029

Product	Discount Rate (%)	Trial Standard Level
Product Class	Discount Rate %	Trial Standard Level
		(billion 2013$)
Hearth Products	3%	1.04

---

[70] OMB Circular A-4, section E (Sept. 17, 2003) (Available at:
http://www.whitehouse.gov/omb/circulars_a004_a-4).

	7%	0.46

The results presented here reflect the use of a flat trend for the price of hearth products over the analysis period (see section IV.F.1).

c. Indirect Impacts on Employment

DOE expects that energy conservation standards for heath products would reduce energy costs for consumers, with the resulting net savings being redirected to other forms of economic activity. Those shifts in spending and economic activity could affect the demand for labor. As described in section IV.N, DOE used an input/output model of the U.S. economy to estimate indirect employment impacts of the TSL that DOE considered in this rulemaking. DOE understands that there are uncertainties involved in projecting employment impacts, especially changes in the later years of the analysis. Therefore, DOE generated results for near-term time frames (2021 to 2026), where these uncertainties are reduced.

The results suggest that the proposed standard would likely have a negligible impact on the net demand for labor in the economy. The net change in jobs is so small that it would be imperceptible in national labor statistics and might be offset by other, unanticipated effects on employment. Chapter 16 of the NOPR TSD presents detailed results regarding indirect employment impacts.

4. Impact on Product Utility or Performance

DOE has tentatively concluded that the standard it is proposing in this NOPR would not lessen the utility or performance of hearth products.

5. Impact of Any Lessening of Competition

DOE considered any lessening of competition that is likely to result from the proposed standard. The Attorney General determines the impact, if any, of any lessening of competition likely to result from a proposed standard, and transmits such determination in writing to the Secretary, together with an analysis of the nature and extent of such impact. To assist the Attorney General in making such determination, DOE has provided DOJ with copies of this NOPR and the TSD for review. DOE will consider DOJ's comments on the proposed rule in preparing the final rule, and DOE will publish and respond to DOJ's comments in that document.

6. Need of the Nation to Conserve Energy

Enhanced energy efficiency, where economically justified, improves the Nation's energy security, strengthens the economy, and reduces the environmental impacts (costs) of energy production and use. Energy savings from energy conservation standards for hearth products covered by this NOPR may also produce environmental benefits in the form of reduced emissions of air pollutants and greenhouse gases. Table V.14 provides DOE's estimate of cumulative emissions reductions projected to result from the TSL considered. The table includes site, power sector, and upstream emissions. The emissions were calculated using the multipliers discussed in section IV.K. DOE reports annual emissions reductions in chapter 13 of the NOPR TSD.

Table V.14. Cumulative Emissions Reduction Estimated for Hearth Products Trial Standard Level

	Trial Standard Level
Site and Power Sector Emissions*	
CO_2 (million metric tons)	32.3
SO_2 (thousand tons)	(4.23)
NO_X (thousand tons)	49.2
Hg (tons)	(0.014)
CH_4 (thousand tons)	0.28
N_2O (thousand tons)	0.01
Upstream Emissions	
CO_2 (million metric tons)	4.78
SO_2 (thousand tons)	(0.03)
NO_X (thousand tons)	75.8
Hg (tons)	(0.000)
CH_4 (thousand tons)	485
N_2O (thousand tons)	0.01
Total FFC Emissions	
CO_2 (million metric tons)	37.0
SO_2 (thousand tons)	(4.26)
NO_X (thousand tons)	125
Hg (tons)	(0.014)
CH_4 (thousand tons)	486
CH_4 (thousand tons CO_2eq)**	13,595
N_2O (thousand tons)	0.01
N_2O (thousand tons CO_2eq)**	3.35

* Primarily site emissions.
** CO_2eq is the quantity of CO_2 that would have the same global warming potential (GWP).
Note: Parentheses indicate negative values.

As part of the analysis for this proposed rule, DOE estimated monetary benefits likely to result from the reduced emissions of CO_2 and NO_X that DOE estimated for the TSL considered for hearth products. As discussed in section IV.L, for CO_2, DOE used the most recent values for the SCC developed by an interagency process. The four sets of

SCC values for CO_2 emissions reductions in 2015 resulting from that process (expressed in 2013$) are represented by \$12.0/metric ton (the average value from a distribution that uses a 5-percent discount rate), \$40.5/metric ton (the average value from a distribution that uses a 3-percent discount rate), \$62.4/metric ton (the average value from a distribution that uses a 2.5-percent discount rate), and \$119/metric ton (the 95th-percentile value from a distribution that uses a 3-percent discount rate). The values for later years are higher due to increasing damages (emissions-related costs) as the projected magnitude of climate change increases.

Table V.15 presents the global value of CO_2 emissions reductions at the considered TSL. DOE calculated a present value of the stream of annual values using the same discount rate as was used in the studies upon which the dollar-per-ton values are based. DOE calculated domestic values as a range from 7 percent to 23 percent of the global values, and these results are presented in chapter 14 of the NOPR TSD.

Table V.15. Estimates of Global Present Value of CO_2 Emissions Reduction Under Hearth Products TSL

TSL	SCC Case*			
	5% discount rate, average	3% discount rate, average	2.5% discount rate, average	3% discount rate, 95th percentile
	million 2013$			
	million 2013$			
Site and Power Sector Emissions				
1	196	956	1,535	2,966
Upstream Emissions				
1	29	142	228	440
Total FFC Emissions				
1	226	1,098	1,763	3,405

* For each of the four cases, the corresponding SCC value for emissions in 2015 is $12.0, $40.5, $62.4, and $119 per metric ton (2013$). The values are for CO_2 only (*i.e.*, not CO_{2eq} of other greenhouse gases).

DOE is well aware that scientific and economic knowledge about the contribution of CO_2 and other greenhouse gas (GHG) emissions to changes in the future global climate and the potential resulting damages to the world economy continues to evolve rapidly. Thus, any value placed on reducing CO_2 emissions in this rulemaking is subject to change. DOE, together with other Federal agencies, will continue to review various methodologies for estimating the monetary value of reductions in CO_2 and other GHG emissions. This ongoing review will consider the comments on this subject that are part of the public record for this and other rulemakings, as well as other methodological assumptions and issues. However, consistent with DOE's legal obligations, and taking into account the uncertainty involved with this particular issue, DOE has included in this proposed rule the most recent values and analyses resulting from the interagency review process.

DOE also estimated a range for the cumulative monetary value of the economic benefits associated with NO_X emissions reductions anticipated to result from the proposed standards for hearth products that are the subject of this NOPR. The dollar-per-ton values that DOE used are discussed in section IV.L. Table V.16 presents the cumulative present values for NO_X emissions reductions for the considered TSL calculated using the average dollar-per-ton value − $2,684 (2013$) − and 7-percent and 3-percent discount rates.

DOE seeks comment on the approach for estimating monetary benefits associated with emissions reductions. This is identified as issue 23 in section VII.E, "Issues on Which DOE Seeks Comment."

Table V.16. Estimates of Present Value of NO_X Emissions Reduction Under the Hearth Products TSL

TSL	3% Discount Rate	7% Discount Rate
	million 2013$	
Site and Power Sector Emissions		
1	58.0	22.8
Upstream Emissions		
1	89.5	35.2
Total FFC Emissions*		
1	148	57.9

* Components may not sum due to rounding.

7. Other Factors

The Secretary of Energy, in determining whether a standard is economically justified, may consider any other factors that the Secretary deems to be relevant. (42 U.S.C. 6295(o)(2)(B)(i)(VI)) No other factors were considered in this analysis.

155

8. Summary of National Economic Impacts

The NPV of the monetized benefits associated with emissions reductions can be viewed as a complement to the NPV of the consumer savings calculated for the new TSL considered in this rulemaking. Table V.17 presents the NPV values that result from adding the estimates of the potential economic benefits resulting from reduced CO_2 and NO_X emissions in each of four valuation scenarios to the NPV of consumer savings calculated for the TSL for hearth products considered in this rulemaking, at both a 7-percent and a 3-percent discount rate. The CO_2 values used in the columns of each table correspond to the four sets of SCC values discussed above.

Table V.17 Hearth Products: Net Present Value of Consumer Savings Combined with Present Value of Monetized Benefits from CO_2 and NO_X Emissions Reductions

TSL	Consumer NPV at 3% Discount Rate added with:			
	SCC Case $12.0/metric ton CO_2^* and Medium Value for NO_X	SCC Case $40.5/metric ton CO_2^* and Medium Value for NO_X	SCC Case $62.4/metric ton CO_2^* and Medium Value for NO_X	SCC Case $119/metric ton CO_2^* and Medium Value for NO_X
	Billion 2013$			
1	3.5	4.4	5.0	6.7
TSL	Consumer NPV at 7% Discount Rate added with:			
	SCC Case $12.0/metric ton CO_2^*	SCC Case $40.5/metric ton CO_2^*	SCC Case $62.4/metric ton CO_2^*	SCC Case $119/metric ton CO_2^*
	Billion 2013$			
1	1.3	2.2	2.9	4.5

* These label values represent the global SCC in 2015, in 2013$. For NO_X emissions, each case uses the medium value, which corresponds to $2,684 per ton.

Although adding the value of consumer savings to the values of emission reductions provides a valuable perspective, two issues should be considered. First, the national operating cost savings are domestic U.S. consumer monetary savings that occur as a result of market transactions, while the value of CO_2 reductions is based on a global

156

value. Second, the assessments of operating cost savings and the SCC are performed with different methods that use different time frames for analysis. The national operating cost savings is measured for the lifetime of products shipped in 2021–2050. The SCC values, on the other hand, reflect the present value of future climate-related impacts resulting from the emission of one metric ton of CO_2 in each year; these impacts continue well beyond 2100.

C. Proposed Standard

When considering proposed standards, the new or amended energy conservation standards that DOE adopts for any type (or class) of covered product, including hearth products, must be designed to achieve the maximum improvement in energy efficiency that is technologically feasible and economically justified. (42 U.S.C. 6295(o)(2)(A)) As discussed previously, in determining whether a standard is economically justified, the Secretary must determine whether the benefits of the standard exceed its burdens by, to the greatest extent practicable, considering the seven statutory factors discussed previously. (42 U.S.C. 6295(o)(2)(B)(i)) The new or amended standard must also "result in significant conservation of energy." (42 U.S.C. 6295(o)(3)(B))

The tables in this section summarize the quantitative analytical results for the considered TSL, based on the assumptions and methodology discussed herein. In addition to the quantitative results presented in the tables, DOE also considers other burdens and benefits that affect economic justification. These include the impacts on identifiable subgroups of consumers who may be disproportionately affected by a national standard (see section V.B.1.b), and impacts on employment. DOE discusses the impacts on direct employment in hearth products manufacturing in section V.B.2.b, and discusses the indirect employment impacts in chapter 16 of the NOPR TSD.

DOE also notes that the economics literature provides a wide-ranging discussion of how consumers trade off upfront costs and energy savings in the absence of government intervention. Much of this literature attempts to explain why consumers appear to undervalue energy efficiency improvements. There is evidence that consumers undervalue future energy savings as a result of: (1) a lack of information; (2) a lack of sufficient salience of the long-term or aggregate benefits; (3) a lack of sufficient savings to warrant delaying or altering purchases; (4) excessive focus on the short term, in the form of inconsistent weighting of future energy cost savings relative to available returns on other investments; (5) computational or other difficulties associated with the evaluation of relevant tradeoffs; and (6) a divergence in incentives (for example, renter versus owner or builder versus purchaser). Other literature indicates that with less than perfect foresight and a high degree of uncertainty about the future, consumers may trade off at a higher than expected rate between current consumption and uncertain future energy cost savings. This undervaluation suggests that regulation that promotes energy efficiency can produce significant net private gains (as well as producing social gains by, for example, reducing pollution).

In DOE's current regulatory analysis, potential changes in the benefits and costs of a regulation due to changes in consumer purchase decisions are included in two ways.

First, if consumers forego a purchase of a product in the standards case, this decreases

sales for product manufacturers and the cost to manufacturers is included in the MIA.

Second, DOE accounts for energy savings attributable only to products actually used by

consumers in the standards case; if a standard decreases the number of products

purchased by consumers, this decreases the potential energy savings from an energy

conservation standard. DOE provides estimates of changes in the volume of product

purchases in chapter 9 of the NOPR TSD. DOE's current analysis does not explicitly

control for heterogeneity in consumer preferences, preferences across subcategories of

products or specific features, or consumer price sensitivity variation according to

household income.[71]

While DOE is not prepared at present to provide a fuller quantifiable framework

for estimating the benefits and costs of changes in consumer purchase decisions due to an

energy conservation standard, DOE is committed to developing a framework that can

support empirical quantitative tools for improved assessment of the consumer welfare

impacts of appliance standards. DOE has posted a paper that discusses the issue of

consumer welfare impacts of appliance standards and potential enhancements to the

methodology by which these impacts are defined and estimated in the regulatory

process.[72] DOE welcomes comments on how to more fully assess the potential impact of

---

[71] P.C. Reiss and M.W. White, Household Electricity Demand, Revisited, Review of Economic Studies (2005) 72, 853–883.
[72] Alan Sanstad, Notes on the Economics of Household Energy Consumption and Technology Choice. Lawrence Berkeley National Laboratory (2010) (Available at: http://www1.eere.energy.gov/buildings/appliance_standards/pdfs/consumer_ee_theory.pdf (Last accessed May 3, 2013).

energy conservation standards on consumer choice and how to quantify this impact in its regulatory analysis.

1. Benefits and Burdens of the Trial Standard Level Considered for Hearth Products

Table V.18 and Table V.19 summarize the quantitative impacts estimated for the potential standard for hearth products. The national impacts are measured over the lifetime of hearth products purchased in the 30-year period that begins in the year of compliance with the considered standard (2021-2050). The energy savings, emissions reductions, and value of emissions reductions refer to FFC results.

Table V.18. Summary of Analytical Results for Hearth Products: National Impacts

Category	TSL 1
National FFC Energy Savings (quads)	
	0.69
NPV of Consumer Benefits (2013$ billion)	
3% discount rate	3.1
7% discount rate	1.0
Cumulative Emissions Reduction (Total FFC Emissions)	
CO_2 (million metric tons)	37.0
SO_2 (thousand tons)	(4.26)
NO_X (thousand tons)	125
Hg (tons)	(0.01)
CH_4 (thousand tons)	486
CH_4 (thousand tons CO_2eq)*	13,595
N_2O (thousand tons)	0.01
N_2O (thousand tons CO_2eq)	3.35
Value of Emissions Reduction (Total FFC Emissions)	
CO_2 (2013$ billion)**	0.226 to 3.405
NO_X – 3% discount rate (2013$ million)	148
NO_X – 7% discount rate (2013$ million)	57.9

* CO_2eq is the quantity of CO_2 that would have the same global warming potential (GWP).
** Range of the economic value of CO_2 reductions is based on estimates of the global benefit of reduced CO_2 emissions.
Note: Parentheses indicate negative values.

Table V.19. Summary of Analytical Results for Hearth Products: Manufacturer and Consumer Impacts

Category	TSL 1
Manufacturer Impacts	
Industry NPV (2013$ million) Base Case = $125.3	122-125.8
Change in Industry NPV (2013$ million)	(3.3) to 0.5
Change in Industry NPV (%)†	(2.6) to 0.4
Consumer Mean LCC Savings (2013$)	
Hearth Products	165
Consumer Simple PBP (years)	
Hearth Products	2.9
Consumer LCC Impacts	
Consumers with Net Cost (%)	23

Note: Parentheses indicate negative values.

At TSL 1, DOE estimates there would be a savings of 0.69 quads of energy, an amount DOE considers significant. TSL 1 has an estimated NPV of consumer benefit of $1.03 billion using a 7-percent discount rate, and $3.12 billion using a 3-percent discount rate.

The cumulative emissions reductions at TSL 1 are 37.0 million metric tons (Mt)[73] of carbon dioxide (CO_2), 486 thousand tons of methane (CH_4), 125 thousand tons of nitrogen oxides (NO_X), and 0.01 thousand tons of nitrous oxide (N_2O). Projected emissions show an increase of 4.26 thousand tons of sulfur dioxide (SO_2) and 0.01 tons of mercury (Hg). The increase is due to increased electricity use associated with the shift to electronic ignition in the subject hearth products. The estimated monetary value of the CO_2 emissions reductions at TSL 1 ranges from $0.226 billion to $3.405 billion.

---

[73] A metric ton is equivalent to 1.1 short tons. Results for emissions other than CO_2 are presented in short tons.

At TSL 1, the average LCC savings are $165. The simple PBP is 2.9 years. The share of consumers experiencing a net LCC cost is 23 percent.

At TSL 1, the projected change in INPV ranges from a decrease of $3.3 million to an increase of $0.5 million. If the decrease of $.3.3 million were to occur, TSL 1 could result in a net loss of up to 2.6 percent of INPV for manufacturers of covered hearth products.

The Secretary tentatively concludes that, at TSL 1 for hearth products, the benefits of energy savings, positive NPV of total consumer benefits at a 3-percent and 7-percent discount rate, average consumer LCC savings, emission reductions, and the estimated monetary value of the emissions reductions outweigh the reduction in industry value and the net LCC cost for a small number of consumers. Accordingly, the Secretary of Energy has tentatively concluded that TSL 1 would save a significant amount of energy and is economically justified. Based upon the above considerations, DOE proposes to adopt as an energy conservation standard the prescriptive design requirement that would disallow the use of continuously-burning pilots (*i.e.*, "standing pilots" or "constant-burning pilots") in hearth products.

2. Summary of Benefits and Costs (Annualized) of the Proposed Standards

The benefits and costs of today's proposed standard can also be expressed in terms of annualized values. The annualized monetary values are the sum of: (1) the annualized national economic value (expressed in 2013$) of the benefits from operating products that meet the proposed standards (consisting primarily of operating cost savings

from using less energy, minus increases in product purchase costs, which is another way

of representing consumer NPV), and (2) the annualized monetary value of the benefits of

emission reductions, including CO_2 emission reductions.[74] The value of CO_2 reductions,

otherwise known as the Social Cost of Carbon (SCC), is calculated using a range of

values per metric ton of CO_2 developed by a recent interagency process.

Although combining the values of operating savings and CO_2 emission reductions

provides a useful perspective, two issues should be considered. First, the national

operating savings are domestic U.S. consumer monetary savings that occur as a result of

market transactions, while the value of CO_2 reductions is based on a global value.

Second, the assessments of operating cost savings and CO_2 savings are performed with

different methods that use different time frames for analysis. The national operating cost

savings is measured for the lifetime of hearth products shipped in 2021 –2050. The SCC

values, on the other hand, reflect the present value of some future climate-related impacts

resulting from the emission of one metric ton of carbon dioxide in each year; these

impacts continue well beyond 2100.

Estimates of annualized benefits and costs of the proposed standards for hearth

products are shown in Table V.20. The results under the primary estimate are as follows.

_____

[74] To convert the time-series of costs and benefits into annualized values, DOE calculated a present value in 2014, the year used for discounting the NPV of total consumer costs and savings. For the benefits, DOE calculated a present value associated with each year's shipments in the year in which the shipments occur (2020, 2030, etc.), and then discounted the present value from each year to 2014. The calculation uses discount rates of 3 and 7 percent for all costs and benefits except for the value of CO_2 reductions, for which DOE used case-specific discount rates. Using the present value, DOE then calculated the fixed annual payment over a 30-year period, starting in the compliance year that yields the same present value.

Using a 7-percent discount rate for benefits and costs other than CO_2 reduction (for which DOE used a 3-percent discount rate along with the average SCC series that uses a 3-percent discount rate ($40.5/t in 2015)), the estimated cost of the hearth products standards proposed in this rule is $61.1 million per year in increased equipment costs, while the estimated benefits are $186 million per year in reduced equipment operating costs, $67 million per year in CO_2 reductions, and $7.0 million per year in reduced NO_X emissions. In this case, the net benefit would amount to $199 million per year.

Using a 3-percent discount rate for all benefits and costs and the average SCC series that uses a 3-percent discount rate ($40.5/t in 2015), the estimated cost of the hearth products standards proposed in this rule is $61.2 million per year in increased equipment costs, while the estimated benefits are $251 million per year in reduced equipment operating costs, $67 million per year in CO_2 reductions, and $9.0 million per year in reduced NO_X emissions. In this case, the net benefit would amount to $266 million per year.

Table V.20. Annualized Benefits and Costs of Proposed Standard (TSL 1) for Hearth Products*

	Discount Rate	Primary Estimate	Low Net Benefits Estimate	High Net Benefits Estimate
		million 2013$/year		
Benefits				
Consumer Operating Cost Savings	7%	186	175	195
	3%	251	235	265
CO_2 Reduction Monetized Value ($12.0/t case)**	5%	20	20	20
CO_2 Reduction Monetized Value ($40.5/t case)**	3%	67	67	67

CO_2 Reduction Monetized Value ($62.4/t case)**	2.5%	98	98	98
CO_2 Reduction Monetized Value ($119/t case)**	3%	207	207	207
NO_X Reduction Monetized Value (at $2,684/ton)**	7%	7.00	7.00	7.00
	3%	8.99	8.99	8.99
Total Benefits†	7% plus CO_2 range	212 to 400	202 to 389	222 to 410
	7%	260	249	269
	3% plus CO_2 range	280 to 468	264 to 452	294 to 482
	3%	327	311	341
Costs				
Consumer Incremental Equipment Costs	7%	61.1	61.1	61.1
	3%	61.2	61.2	61.2
Net Benefits				
Total†	7% plus CO_2 range	151 to 339	141 to 328	161 to 349
	7%	199	188	208
	3% plus CO_2 range	219 to 407	203 to 390	233 to 420
	3%	266	250	280

* This table presents the annualized costs and benefits associated with hearth products shipped in 2021−2050. These results include benefits to consumers that accrue after 2050 from the products purchased in 2021−2050. The results account for the incremental variable and fixed costs incurred by manufacturers due to the standard, some of which may be incurred in preparation for the rule. The Primary, Low Benefits, and High Benefits Estimates utilize projections of energy prices from the AEO 2014 Reference case, Low Economic Growth case, and High Economic Growth case, respectively. Incremental product costs are the same in each Estimate.

** The interagency group selected four sets of SCC values for use in regulatory analyses. Three sets of values are based on the average SCC from the three integrated assessment models, at discount rates of 2.5, 3, and 5 percent. The fourth set, which represents the 95th percentile SCC estimate across all three models at a 3-percent discount rate, is included to represent higher-than-expected impacts from temperature change further out in the tails of the SCC distribution. The values in parentheses represent the SCC in 2015. The SCC time series incorporate an escalation factor. The value for NO_X is the average of the low and high values used in DOE's analysis.

† Total benefits for both the 3-percent and 7-percent cases are derived using the series corresponding to average SCC with a 3-percent discount rate ($40.5/t in 2015). In the rows labeled "7% plus CO_2 range" and "3% plus CO_2 range," the operating cost and NO_X benefits are calculated using the labeled discount rate, and those values are added to the full range of CO_2 values.

VI. Procedural Issues and Regulatory Review

A. Review Under Executive Orders 12866 and 13563

Section 1(b)(1) of Executive Order 12866, "Regulatory Planning and Review," 58 FR 51735 (Oct. 4, 1993), requires each agency to identify the problem that it intends to address, including, where applicable, the failures of private markets or public institutions that warrant new agency action, as well as to assess the significance of that problem. The problems these proposed standards address are as follows:

(1) A lack of consumer information and difficulties in analyzing relevant information leads some consumers to miss opportunities to make cost-effective investments in energy efficiency.

(2) In some cases, the benefits of more-efficient products are not realized due to misaligned incentives between purchasers and users. An example of such a case is when the product purchase decision is made by a building contractor or building owner who does not pay the energy costs.

(3) There are external benefits resulting from improved energy efficiency of hearth products that are not captured by the users of such products. These benefits include externalities related to public health, environmental protection, and national security that are not reflected in energy prices, such as reduced emissions of air pollutants and greenhouse gases that impact human health and global warming.

In addition, DOE has determined that this regulatory action is a "significant regulatory action" under section 3(f)(1) of Executive Order 12866. Accordingly, section 6(a)(3) of the Executive Order requires that DOE prepare a regulatory impact analysis (RIA) on this rule and that the Office of Information and Regulatory Affairs (OIRA) in the Office of Management and Budget (OMB) review this rule. DOE presented to OIRA for review the draft rule and other documents prepared for this rulemaking, including the

RIA, and has included these documents in the rulemaking record. The assessments prepared pursuant to Executive Order 12866 can be found in the technical support document for this rulemaking.

DOE has also reviewed this regulation pursuant to Executive Order 13563. 76 FR 3281 (Jan. 21, 2011). Executive Order 13563 is supplemental to and explicitly reaffirms the principles, structures, and definitions governing regulatory review established in Executive Order 12866. To the extent permitted by law, agencies are required by Executive Order 13563 to: (1) propose or adopt a regulation only upon a reasoned determination that its benefits justify its costs (recognizing that some benefits and costs are difficult to quantify); (2) tailor regulations to impose the least burden on society, consistent with obtaining regulatory objectives, taking into account, among other things, and to the extent practicable, the costs of cumulative regulations; (3) select, in choosing among alternative regulatory approaches, those approaches that maximize net benefits (including potential economic, environmental, public health and safety, and other advantages; distributive impacts; and equity); (4) to the extent feasible, specify performance objectives, rather than specifying the behavior or manner of compliance that regulated entities must adopt; and (5) identify and assess available alternatives to direct regulation, including providing economic incentives to encourage the desired behavior, such as user fees or marketable permits, or providing information upon which choices can be made by the public.

DOE emphasizes as well that Executive Order 13563 requires agencies to use the best available techniques to quantify anticipated present and future benefits and costs as accurately as possible. In its guidance, the Office of Information and Regulatory Affairs has emphasized that such techniques may include identifying changing future compliance costs that might result from technological innovation or anticipated behavioral changes. For the reasons stated in the preamble, DOE believes that this NOPR is consistent with these principles, including the requirement that, to the extent permitted by law, benefits justify costs and that net benefits are maximized.

B. Review Under the Regulatory Flexibility Act

The Regulatory Flexibility Act (5 U.S.C. 601 *et seq.*) requires preparation of an initial regulatory flexibility analysis (IRFA) for any rule that by law must be proposed for public comment, unless the agency certifies that the rule, if promulgated, will not have a significant economic impact on a substantial number of small entities. As required by Executive Order 13272, "Proper Consideration of Small Entities in Agency Rulemaking," 67 FR 53461 (August 16, 2002), DOE published procedures and policies on February 19, 2003, to ensure that the potential impacts of its rules on small entities are properly considered during the rulemaking process. 68 FR 7990. DOE has made its procedures and policies available on the Office of the General Counsel's website (http://energy.gov/gc/office-general-counsel). DOE has prepared the following IRFA for the products that are the subject of this rulemaking.

For manufacturers of gas hearth products, the Small Business Administration (SBA) has set a size threshold, which defines those entities classified as "small businesses" for the purposes of the statute. DOE used the SBA's small business size standards to determine whether any small entities would be subject to the requirements of the rule. 65 FR 30836, 30848 (May 15, 2000), as amended at 65 FR 53533, 53544 (Sept. 5, 2000) and codified at 13 CFR part 121. The size standards are listed by North American Industry Classification System (NAICS) code and industry description and are available at http://www.sba.gov/sites/default/files/files/Size_Standards_Table.pdf. Manufacturing of heating hearth products is classified under NAICS code 333414, "Heating Equipment (Except Warm Air Furnaces) Manufacturing," and manufacturing of decorative hearth products is classified under NAICS code 335228, "Other Major Household Appliance Manufacturing." For both NAICS codes, the SBA sets a threshold of 500 employees or fewer for an entity to be considered a small business. This 500-employee threshold includes all employees in a business's parent company and any other subsidiaries.

1. Description and Estimated Number of Small Entities Regulated

   a. Methodology for Estimating the Number of Small Entities

DOE reviewed the potential standard levels considered in today's NOPR under the provisions of the Regulatory Flexibility Act and the procedures and policies published on February 19, 2003. To better assess the potential impacts of this rulemaking on small entities, DOE conducted a more focused inquiry of the companies that could be small business manufacturers of products covered by this rulemaking. During its market survey, DOE used publicly-available information to identify potential small manufacturers. DOE's research involved industry trade association membership directories (*e.g.*, HPBA), information from previous rulemakings, individual company websites, and market research tools (*e.g.*, Hoover's reports) to create a list of companies that manufacture gas hearth products covered by this rulemaking. DOE also asked stakeholders and industry representatives if they were aware of any additional small manufacturers during manufacturer interviews. DOE reviewed publicly-available data and contacted various companies on its complete list of manufacturers to determine whether they met the SBA's definition of a small business manufacturer of gas hearth products. DOE screened out companies that do not manufacture products impacted by this rulemaking, do not meet the definition of a "small business," or are foreign owned and operated.

DOE identified 90 potential manufacturers of gas hearth products sold in the U.S. that would be affected by today's proposal. Of these, DOE identified 66 as domestic small business manufacturers. DOE contacted a subset of small businesses to invite them to take part in a manufacturer impact analysis interview. Of 25 small businesses contacted, DOE was able to reach and discuss potential standards with five of those entities. DOE also obtained information about small businesses and potential impacts on small businesses while interviewing large manufacturers.

In interviews, small manufacturers expressed concern regarding the impact of disallowing standing pilot lights on their ability to compete with larger manufacturers. Manufacturers stated that gas hearth products with electronic ignition systems cost more to produce than gas hearth products with standing pilot lights, as the components purchased for electronic ignition systems tend to be more expensive. Since large manufacturers often produce at higher volumes, they may be able to source components at lower per-unit prices than small manufacturers that produce at lower volumes. Because small manufacturers may not benefit from the same economies of scale as large manufacturers, an energy conservation standard disallowing standing pilot lights could disproportionately impact their production costs and, in turn, the prices at which they sell their products. This anticipated change in manufacturer production costs (MPCs) drove small manufacturer concerns surrounding the impact of an energy conservation standard on their ability to remain competitive in the gas hearth market.

2. Description and Estimate of Compliance Requirements

To evaluate small manufacturers' concerns regarding the competitive implications of disallowing standing pilot lights, DOE modeled the difference in cost small manufacturers might face when sourcing components at lower volumes. Due to limited available information on the relative sales volumes of small and large manufacturers, DOE selected volumes of 1,000 units (used to represent small manufacturers) and 10,000 units (used to represent large manufacturers) for each product group analyzed. DOE developed its analysis based on the engineering teardown analysis and cost model, as well as manufacturer feedback on the costs of electronic ignition systems.

The table below presents the estimated added per-unit cost of an electronic ignition system compared to a standing pilot system at the two representative production volumes modeled. As the results indicate, manufacturers would likely pay less per unit

171

when producing 10,000 units versus 1,000 units. Estimated costs would be expected to decline further as production volumes climb higher.

Table VI.1 Added Cost of Electronic Ignition Systems at Representative Production Volumes

Product Group	Baseline MPC	Added Cost at 1,000 units	Added Cost at 10,000 units
Vented Fireplace/ Insert/ Stove	$322	$31	$26
Unvented Fireplace/Insert /Stove	$281	$33	$24
Vented Log Sets	$190	$70	$58
Unvented Log Sets	$208	$69	$51
Outdoor Hearths	$210	$65	$42

DOE's analysis suggests that disallowing standing pilot lights would increase the per-unit MPCs of gas hearth products by a greater amount for small-volume producers than for large-volume producers. Higher MPCs, in turn, typically lead to higher end-user purchase prices. If products manufactured by small businesses cannot compete with products manufactured by large businesses at lower cost, small businesses could potentially experience a decline in profits and/or choose to exit the market.

DOE recognizes that larger manufacturers may have a competitive advantage due to their size and ability to source purchased parts at lower cost. If the per-unit cost of products increases more for small manufacturers than for large manufacturers, and if small manufacturers are not able to pass costs through to price-sensitive consumers, they could potentially face reduced markups and profits, as well as a decline in market share. Because the proposed standard could cause competitive concerns for small manufacturers, DOE cannot certify that the proposed standard would not have a significant impact on a substantial number of small businesses.

3. Duplication, Overlap, and Conflict with Other Rules and Regulations

DOE is not aware of any rules or regulations that duplicate, overlap, or conflict with the rule being considered today.

4. Significant Alternatives to the Rule

DOE is required by EPCA to establish standards that achieve the maximum improvement in energy efficiency that is technically feasible and economically justified and results in a significant conservation of energy. The discussion above analyzes impacts on small businesses that would result from the ban on standing pilot lights that DOE is proposing in today's notice. In addition to the ban on standing pilot lights being considered, the NOPR TSD includes a regulatory impact analysis (RIA) in chapter 17. For gas hearth products, the RIA discusses the following policy alternatives: (1) no change in standard; (2) consumer rebates; (3) consumer tax credits; (4) manufacturer tax credits; (5) voluntary energy efficiency targets; and (6) government bulk purchases. While these alternatives may mitigate to some varying extent the economic impacts on small entities compared to the proposed standards, DOE does not intend to consider these alternatives further because in several cases, they would not be feasible to implement without authority and funding from Congress, and in all cases, DOE has determined that the site energy savings of these alternatives are significantly smaller than those that would be expected to result from adoption of the proposed standard (ranging from approximately 0.0 0percent to 15.9 percent of the site energy savings from the proposed standard). Accordingly, DOE is declining to adopt any of these alternatives and is proposing the standard set forth in this rulemaking. (See chapter 17 of the NOPR TSD for further detail on the policy alternatives DOE considered.)

DOE continues to seek input from small businesses that would be affected by this rulemaking and will consider comments received in the development of any final rule.

C. Review Under the Paperwork Reduction Act of 1995

Manufacturers of hearth products must certify to DOE that their products comply with any applicable energy conservation standards. DOE has established regulations for the certification and recordkeeping requirements for all covered consumer products and commercial equipment (76 FR 12422 (March 7, 2011)) and plans to establish such regulations for hearth products pending the outcome of the proposed determination of coverage and energy conservation standards rulemakings. The collection-of-information requirement for the certification and recordkeeping is subject to review and approval by OMB under the Paperwork Reduction Act (PRA). DOE will seek OMB approval under the PRA in the rulemaking that establishes the certification requirements for hearth products, which will be conducted subsequent to the current proceeding if the proposed determination is ultimately positive and energy conservation standards are ultimately adopted.

Notwithstanding any other provision of the law, no person is required to respond to, nor shall any person be subject to a penalty for failure to comply with, a collection of information subject to the requirements of the PRA, unless that collection of information displays a currently valid OMB Control Number.

D. Review Under the National Environmental Policy Act of 1969

Pursuant to the National Environmental Policy Act (NEPA) of 1969, DOE has determined that the proposed rule fits within the category of actions included in Categorical Exclusion (CX) B5.1 and otherwise meets the requirements for application of a CX. See 10 CFR Part 1021, App. B, B5.1(b); 1021.410(b) and Appendix B, B(1)-(5). The proposed rule fits within the category of actions because it is a rulemaking that establishes energy conservation standards for consumer products or industrial equipment, and for which none of the exceptions identified in CX B5.1(b) apply. Therefore, DOE has made a CX determination for this rulemaking, and DOE does not need to prepare an Environmental Assessment or Environmental Impact Statement for this proposed rule. DOE's CX determination for this proposed rule is available at http://cxnepa.energy.gov/.

E. Review Under Executive Order 13132

Executive Order 13132, "Federalism," 64 FR 43255 (Aug. 10, 1999), imposes certain requirements on Federal agencies formulating and implementing policies or regulations that preempt State law or that have Federalism implications. The Executive Order requires agencies to examine the constitutional and statutory authority supporting any action that would limit the policymaking discretion of the States and to carefully assess the necessity for such actions. The Executive Order also requires agencies to have an accountable process to ensure meaningful and timely input by State and local officials in the development of regulatory policies that have Federalism implications. On March 14, 2000, DOE published a statement of policy describing the intergovernmental consultation process it will follow in the development of such regulations. 65 FR 13735. DOE has examined this proposed rule and has tentatively determined that it would not have a substantial direct effect on the States, on the relationship between the national government and the States, or on the distribution of power and responsibilities among the various levels of government. EPCA governs and prescribes Federal preemption of State regulations as to energy conservation for the products that are the subject of this proposed rule. States can petition DOE for exemption from such preemption to the extent, and based on criteria, set forth in EPCA. (42 U.S.C. 6297) Therefore, no further action is required by Executive Order 13132.

F. Review Under Executive Order 12988

With respect to the review of existing regulations and the promulgation of new regulations, section 3(a) of Executive Order 12988, "Civil Justice Reform," imposes on Federal agencies the general duty to adhere to the following requirements: (1) eliminate drafting errors and ambiguity; (2) write regulations to minimize litigation; (3) provide a clear legal standard for affected conduct rather than a general standard; and (4) promote simplification and burden reduction. 61 FR 4729 (Feb. 7, 1996). Regarding the review required by section 3(a), section 3(b) of Executive Order 12988 specifically requires that Executive agencies make every reasonable effort to ensure that the regulation: (1) clearly specifies the preemptive effect, if any; (2) clearly specifies any effect on existing Federal law or regulation; (3) provides a clear legal standard for affected conduct while promoting simplification and burden reduction; (4) specifies the retroactive effect, if any; (5) adequately defines key terms; and (6) addresses other important issues affecting clarity and general draftsmanship under any guidelines issued by the Attorney General. Section 3(c) of Executive Order 12988 requires Executive agencies to review regulations in light of applicable standards in section 3(a) and section 3(b) to determine whether they are met or it is unreasonable to meet one or more of them. DOE has completed the required review and determined that, to the extent permitted by law, this proposed rule meets the relevant standards of Executive Order 12988.

G. Review Under the Unfunded Mandates Reform Act of 1995

Title II of the Unfunded Mandates Reform Act of 1995 (UMRA) requires each Federal agency to assess the effects of Federal regulatory actions on State, local, and Tribal governments and the private sector. Pub. L. 104-4, sec. 201 (codified at 2 U.S.C. 1531). For a proposed regulatory action likely to result in a rule that may cause the expenditure by State, local, and Tribal governments, in the aggregate, or by the private sector of $100 million or more in any one year (adjusted annually for inflation), section 202 of UMRA requires a Federal agency to publish a written statement that estimates the resulting costs, benefits, and other effects on the national economy. (2 U.S.C. 1532(a), (b)) The UMRA also requires a Federal agency to develop an effective process to permit timely input by elected officers of State, local, and Tribal governments on a proposed "significant intergovernmental mandate," and requires an agency plan for giving notice and opportunity for timely input to potentially affected small governments before establishing any requirements that might significantly or uniquely affect them. On March

18, 1997, DOE published a statement of policy on its process for intergovernmental

consultation under UMRA. 62 FR 12820. DOE's policy statement is also available at

http://energy.gov/gc/office-general-counsel.

Although this proposed rule, which proposes energy conservation standards for

hearth products, does not contain a Federal intergovernmental mandate, it may require

expenditures of $100 million or more on the private sector. Specifically, the proposed

rule would likely result in a final rule that could require expenditures of $100 million or

more, including: (1) investment in research and development and in capital expenditures

by residential hearth product manufacturers in the years between the final rule and the

compliance date for the new standards, and (2) incremental additional expenditures by

consumers to purchase higher-efficiency hearth products, starting at the compliance date

for the applicable standard.

Section 202 of UMRA authorizes a Federal agency to respond to the content

requirements of UMRA in any other statement or analysis that accompanies the proposed

rule. (2 U.S.C. 1532(c)) The content requirements of section 202(b) of UMRA relevant

to a private sector mandate substantially overlap the economic analysis requirements that

apply under section 325(o) of EPCA and Executive Order 12866. The

SUPPLEMENTARY INFORMATION section of the NOPR and the "Regulatory

Impact Analysis" section of the TSD for this proposed rule respond to those

requirements.

Under section 205 of UMRA, the Department is obligated to identify and consider a reasonable number of regulatory alternatives before promulgating a rule for which a written statement under section 202 is required. (2 U.S.C. 1535(a)) DOE is required to select from those alternatives the most cost-effective and least burdensome alternative that achieves the objectives of the proposed rule unless DOE publishes an explanation for doing otherwise, or the selection of such an alternative is inconsistent with law. Pursuant to 42 U.S.C. 6292(a)(20) and (b)(1) and 42 U.S.C. 6295(l)(1)-(2) and (o), this proposed rule would establish amended energy conservation standards for hearth products that are designed to achieve the maximum improvement in energy efficiency that DOE has determined to be both technologically feasible and economically justified. A full discussion of the alternatives considered by DOE is presented in the "Regulatory Impact Analysis" section of the TSD for this proposed rule.

H. Review Under the Treasury and General Government Appropriations Act, 1999

Section 654 of the Treasury and General Government Appropriations Act, 1999 (Pub. L. 105-277) requires Federal agencies to issue a Family Policymaking Assessment for any rule that may affect family well-being. This rule would not have any impact on the autonomy or integrity of the family as an institution. Accordingly, DOE has concluded that it is not necessary to prepare a Family Policymaking Assessment.

I. Review Under Executive Order 12630

Pursuant to Executive Order 12630, "Governmental Actions and Interference with Constitutionally Protected Property Rights," 53 FR 8859 (March 15, 1988), DOE has determined that this proposed rule would not result in any takings that might require compensation under the Fifth Amendment to the U.S. Constitution.

J. Review Under the Treasury and General Government Appropriations Act, 2001

Section 515 of the Treasury and General Government Appropriations Act, 2001 (44 U.S.C. 3516 note) provides for Federal agencies to review most disseminations of information to the public under information quality guidelines established by each agency pursuant to general guidelines issued by OMB. OMB's guidelines were published at 67 FR 8452 (Feb. 22, 2002), and DOE's guidelines were published at 67 FR 62446 (Oct. 7, 2002). DOE has reviewed this NOPR under the OMB and DOE guidelines and has concluded that it is consistent with applicable policies in those guidelines.

K. Review Under Executive Order 13211

Executive Order 13211, "Actions Concerning Regulations That Significantly Affect Energy Supply, Distribution, or Use," 66 FR 28355 (May 22, 2001), requires Federal agencies to prepare and submit to OIRA at OMB, a Statement of Energy Effects for any proposed significant energy action. A "significant energy action" is defined as any action by an agency that promulgates or is expected to lead to promulgation of a final rule, and that: (1) is a significant regulatory action under Executive Order 12866, or any successor order; and (2) is likely to have a significant adverse effect on the supply, distribution, or use of energy, or (3) is designated by the Administrator of OIRA as a significant energy action. For any proposed significant energy action, the agency must give a detailed statement of any adverse effects on energy supply, distribution, or use should the proposal be implemented, and of reasonable alternatives to the action and their expected benefits on energy supply, distribution, and use.

DOE has tentatively concluded that this regulatory action, which would adopt energy conservation standards for hearth products, is not a significant energy action because the proposed standards are not likely to have a significant adverse effect on the supply, distribution, or use of energy, nor has it been designated as such by the Administrator at OIRA. Accordingly, DOE has not prepared a Statement of Energy Effects on this proposed rule.

L. Review Under the Information Quality Bulletin for Peer Review

On December 16, 2004, OMB, in consultation with the Office of Science and Technology Policy (OSTP), issued its Final Information Quality Bulletin for Peer Review (the Bulletin). 70 FR 2664 (Jan. 14, 2005). The Bulletin establishes that certain scientific information shall be peer reviewed by qualified specialists before it is disseminated by the Federal Government, including influential scientific information related to agency regulatory actions. The purpose of the bulletin is to enhance the quality and credibility of the Government's scientific information. Under the Bulletin, the energy conservation standards rulemaking analyses are "influential scientific information," which the Bulletin defines as "scientific information the agency reasonably can determine will have or does have a clear and substantial impact on important public policies or private sector decisions." Id. at 2667.

In response to OMB's Bulletin, DOE conducted formal in-progress peer reviews of the energy conservation standards development process and analyses and has prepared a Peer Review Report pertaining to the energy conservation standards rulemaking analyses. Generation of this report involved a rigorous, formal, and documented evaluation using objective criteria and qualified and independent reviewers to make a judgment as to the technical/scientific/business merit, the actual or anticipated results, and the productivity and management effectiveness of programs and/or projects. The "Energy Conservation Standards Rulemaking Peer Review Report," dated February 2007, has been disseminated and is available at the following Web site: www1.eere.energy.gov/buildings/appliance_standards/peer_review.html.

VII. Public Participation

A. Attendance at the Public Meeting

The time, date, and location of the public meeting are listed in the **DATES** and **ADDRESSES** sections at the beginning of this notice. If you plan to attend the public meeting, please notify Ms. Brenda Edwards at (202) 586-2945 or Brenda.Edwards@ee.doe.gov. As explained in the **ADDRESSES** section, foreign nationals visiting DOE Headquarters are subject to advance security screening procedures. Any foreign national wishing to participate in the meeting should advise DOE of this fact as soon as possible by contacting Ms. Brenda Edwards to initiate the necessary procedures.

In addition, you can attend the public meeting via webinar. Webinar registration information, participant instructions, and information about the capabilities available to webinar participants will be published on DOE's website at:

http://www1.eere.energy.gov/buildings/appliance_standards/rulemaking.aspx?ruleid=84

Participants are responsible for ensuring their systems are compatible with the webinar software.

B. Procedure for Submitting Requests to Speak and Prepared General Statements For Distribution

Any person who has an interest in the topics addressed in this notice, or who is representative of a group or class of persons that has an interest in these issues, may request an opportunity to make an oral presentation at the public meeting. Such persons may hand-deliver requests to speak to the address shown in the **ADDRESSES** section at the beginning of this notice between 9:00 a.m. and 4:00 p.m., Monday through Friday, except Federal holidays. Requests may also be sent by mail or email to: Ms. Brenda Edwards, U.S. Department of Energy, Building Technologies Office, Mailstop EE-5B, 1000 Independence Avenue, SW, Washington, DC 20585-0121, or Brenda.Edwards@ee.doe.gov. Persons who wish to speak should include with their request a computer diskette or CD-ROM in WordPerfect, Microsoft Word, PDF, or text (ASCII) file format that briefly describes the nature of their interest in this rulemaking and the topics they wish to discuss. Such persons should also provide a daytime telephone number where they can be reached.

DOE requests persons scheduled to make an oral presentation to submit an advance copy of their statements at least one week before the public meeting. DOE may permit persons who cannot supply an advance copy of their statement to participate, if those persons have made advance alternative arrangements with the Building Technologies Program. As necessary, requests to give an oral presentation should ask for such alternative arrangements.

C. Conduct of the Public Meeting

DOE will designate a DOE official to preside at the public meeting and may also use a professional facilitator to aid discussion. The meeting will not be a judicial or evidentiary-type public hearing, but DOE will conduct it in accordance with section 336 of EPCA (42 U.S.C. 6306). A court reporter will be present to record the proceedings and prepare a transcript. DOE reserves the right to schedule the order of presentations and to establish the procedures governing the conduct of the public meeting. There shall not be discussion of proprietary information, costs or prices, market share, or other commercial matters regulated by U.S. anti-trust laws. After the public meeting, interested parties may submit further comments on the proceedings, as well as on any aspect of the rulemaking, until the end of the comment period.

The public meeting will be conducted in an informal, conference style. DOE will present summaries of comments received before the public meeting, allow time for prepared general statements by participants, and encourage all interested parties to share their views on issues affecting this rulemaking. Each participant will be allowed to make a general statement (within time limits determined by DOE), before the discussion of specific topics. DOE will allow, as time permits, other participants to comment briefly on any general statements.

At the end of all prepared statements on a topic, DOE will permit participants to clarify their statements briefly and comment on statements made by others. Participants should be prepared to answer questions by DOE and by other participants concerning these issues. DOE representatives may also ask questions of participants concerning other matters relevant to this rulemaking. The official conducting the public meeting will accept additional comments or questions from those attending, as time permits. The presiding official will announce any further procedural rules or modification of the above procedures that may be needed for the proper conduct of the public meeting.

A transcript of the public meeting will be included in the docket, which can be viewed as described in the Docket section at the beginning of this notice and will be accessible on the DOE website. In addition, any person may buy a copy of the transcript from the transcribing reporter.

D. Submission of Comments

DOE will accept comments, data, and information regarding this proposed rule before or after the public meeting, but no later than the date provided in the **DATES** section at the beginning of this proposed rule. Interested parties may submit comments, data, and other information using any of the methods described in the **ADDRESSES** section at the beginning of this notice.

Submitting comments via www.regulations.gov. The www.regulations.gov webpage will require you to provide your name and contact information. Your contact information will be viewable to DOE Building Technologies staff only. Your contact information will not be publicly viewable except for your first and last names, organization name (if any), and submitter representative name (if any). If your comment is not processed properly because of technical difficulties, DOE will use this information to contact you. If DOE cannot read your comment due to technical difficulties and cannot contact you for clarification, DOE may not be able to consider your comment.

However, your contact information will be publicly viewable if you include it in the comment itself or in any documents attached to your comment. Any information that you do not want to be publicly viewable should not be included in your comment, nor in any document attached to your comment. Otherwise, persons viewing comments will see only first and last names, organization names, correspondence containing comments, and any documents submitted with the comments.

Do not submit to www.regulations.gov information for which disclosure is restricted by statute, such as trade secrets and commercial or financial information (hereinafter referred to as Confidential Business Information (CBI)). Comments submitted through www.regulations.gov cannot be claimed as CBI. Comments received through the website will waive any CBI claims for the information submitted. For information on submitting CBI, see the Confidential Business Information section below.

DOE processes submissions made through www.regulations.gov before posting. Normally, comments will be posted within a few days of being submitted. However, if large volumes of comments are being processed simultaneously, your comment may not be viewable for up to several weeks. Please keep the comment tracking number that www.regulations.gov provides after you have successfully uploaded your comment.

Submitting comments via email, hand delivery/courier, or mail. Comments and documents submitted via email, hand delivery, or mail also will be posted to www.regulations.gov. If you do not want your personal contact information to be publicly viewable, do not include it in your comment or any accompanying documents. Instead, provide your contact information in a cover letter. Include your first and last names, email address, telephone number, and optional mailing address. The cover letter will not be publicly viewable as long as it does not include any comments

Include contact information each time you submit comments, data, documents, and other information to DOE. If you submit via mail or hand delivery/courier, please provide all items on a CD, if feasible, in which case, it is not necessary to submit printed copies. No telefacsimiles (faxes) will be accepted.

Comments, data, and other information submitted to DOE electronically should be provided in PDF (preferred), Microsoft Word or Excel, WordPerfect, or text (ASCII) file format. Provide documents that are not secured, that are written in English, and that are free of any defects or viruses. Documents should not contain special characters or any form of encryption and, if possible, they should carry the electronic signature of the author.

Campaign form letters. Please submit campaign form letters by the originating organization in batches of between 50 to 500 form letters per PDF or as one form letter with a list of supporters' names compiled into one or more PDFs. This reduces comment processing and posting time.

Confidential Business Information. Pursuant to 10 CFR 1004.11, any person submitting information that he or she believes to be confidential and exempt by law from public disclosure should submit via email, postal mail, or hand delivery/courier two well-marked copies: one copy of the document marked "confidential" including all the information believed to be confidential, and one copy of the document marked "non-confidential" with the information believed to be confidential deleted. Submit these documents via email or on a CD, if feasible. DOE will make its own determination about the confidential status of the information and treat it according to its determination.

Factors of interest to DOE when evaluating requests to treat submitted information as confidential include: (1) A description of the items; (2) whether and why such items are customarily treated as confidential within the industry; (3) whether the information is generally known by or available from other sources; (4) whether the information has previously been made available to others without obligation concerning its confidentiality; (5) an explanation of the competitive injury to the submitting person which would result from public disclosure; (6) when such information might lose its confidential character due to the passage of time; and (7) why disclosure of the information would be contrary to the public interest.

It is DOE's policy that all comments may be included in the public docket, without change and as received, including any personal information provided in the comments (except information deemed to be exempt from public disclosure).

E. Issues on Which DOE Seeks Comment

Although DOE welcomes comments on any aspect of this proposal, DOE is particularly interested in receiving comments and views of interested parties concerning the following issues:

1. DOE seeks comment on the proposed definition for hearth products found in the December 2013 NOPD (78 FR 79638) and the range of products covered by the proposed rule if this definition were applied in the final rulemaking. DOE requests comment on which products would fall into each of the product groups as currently defined (1. vented fireplaces/stoves/inserts, 2. unvented fireplaces/stoves, inserts, 3. vented

gas log sets, 4. unvented gas log sets, and 5. outdoor) and whether additional clarifying criteria should be added to the definition to cover intended products. DOE requests comment on which hearth products that are "gas appliances that simulate a solid-fueled fireplace or presents a flame pattern" may by the proposed definition be grouped into the hearth product category, but may warrant a different design standard due to such factors as utility of the feature to users. (See section III.A.)

2. DOE seeks input on the assumption that should standing pilot ignitions be disallowed, electronic intermittent ignitions would provide the same level of safety as a standing pilot and whether a standing pilot provides a means for ensuring that gas is lit prior to opening the gas valve and ensuring that oxygen levels in a the room remain at a safe levels prior to the main burner ignition. DOE request comment on whether there are any ANSI safety standard certification, building code, or other industry safety standard that may preclude a manufacturer from selling a particular hearth product with an electronic intermittent ignition. (See section III.B.)

3. DOE seeks comment on its tentative conclusions regarding hearth product definitions and categorizations as they pertain to active mode energy use. (See section III.C and chapter 3 of the TSD.)

4. DOE seeks comment on its screening analysis including any potential impacts on product utility or availability. (See section III.G.1.d and chapter 4 of the TSD.)

5. DOE seeks comment on its assumptions regarding the electrical energy consumption of the ignition module for hearth products. (See section III.I and chapter 7 of the TSD).

6. DOE seeks comment on its list of identified technologies for reducing the fuel consumption of hearth products. (See section IV.A.3 and chapter 3 of the TSD.)

7. DOE seeks comment on its general engineering analysis approach for hearth products. (See section IV.C and chapter 5 of the TSD.)

8. DOE seeks comment on the availability and applicability of intermittent pilot ignition components for hearth products. (See section IV.C.1 and chapter 5 of the TSD.)

9. DOE requests comment on its assumption that ignition component costs for vented fireplaces, inserts, and stoves are equivalent. (See section IV.C.1 and chapter 5 of the TSD.)

10. DOE requests comment on the derived manufacturer production costs and markups. (See sections IV.C.3.e and IV.C.4 and chapter 5 of the TSD.)

11. DOE seeks input on the representative input capacities (kBtu/h) used to calculate the fuel used by the standing pilot for each of the five hearth product groups identified in the proposal and discussed in Chapter 7 of the TSD. In particular, the agency seeks input on whether the RECS 2009 annual space heating energy consumption numbers for vented and unvented fireplaces is representative of all hearth products and any data that would be helpful in estimating the energy consumption for the hearth

product groups identified. DOE also seeks comment on the average on-time per cycle assumption of 30 seconds for intermittent pilot ignition and any data indicating specific on-time per cycle for different product groups to help inform the energy use analysis. (See section IV.E and chapter 7 of the TSD.)

12. DOE requests comment on the assumed pilot light usage, specifically the percentages of consumers who operate their hearth product standing pilots year round, for only the heating season, only when operating the unit, the treatment of LPG units, and the treatment of heat input into the space by the standing pilot. (See section IV.E and chapter 7 of the TSD.)

13. DOE requests comment on the assumption to not apply a trend to its manufacturer selling price, as well as any information that would support the use of alternate assumptions. (See section IV.F.1 and chapter 8 of the TSD.)

14. DOE requests comment on installation and retrofit assumptions regarding electrical connections and grounding. (See section IV.F.1 and chapter 8 of the TSD.)

15. DOE requests comment on intermittent pilot ignition module repair frequency and cost components applied in the life-cycle cost and payback period analysis. The agency requests input on the use of $142.89 as the bare material cost of repair of the intermittent pilot compared the bare material cost of a standing pilot of $43.72. In addition, the agency requests comment on the labor hours associated with the repair of both the

standing pilot and intermittent pilot, which were both determined to be 1.50 labor hours as referenced in Section 8.2.3.2 of the TSD. DOE also requests comment on whether consumers may choose to replace the entire product as opposed to repair the failed ignition device and at what price point consumers would make that decision and for which hearth products. (See section IV.F.2.c and chapter 8 of the TSD.)

16. DOE requests comment on lifetime assumptions applied in the life-cycle cost and payback period analysis where DOE assumes the minimum lifetime of both the hearth product and ignition system to be 5 years and 1 year, respectively and that for purposes of the life-cycle cost analysis that any repair costs would be free to the consumer during this warranty period. In addition, DOE requests comment on the product lifetime distribution for hearth products that are average are assumed to be 15 years and for hearth product ignition systems are assumed to be 7.3 years as laid out in Section 8.2.3.3 of the TSD. DOE requests input on lifetime for products identified in the five different hearth product groups (vented fireplaces, unvented fireplaces, vented log sets, unvented log sets, and outdoor) that may inform the lifetime distribution analysis. (See section IV.F.2.d and chapter 8 of the TSD.)

17. DOE requests comment on the estimated base-case efficiency distribution. (See section IV.F.2.f and chapter 8 of the TSD.)

18. DOE requests comment on its assumption that switching from gas to electric hearth products due to the imposition of the design standard would be negligible. (See section IV.G and chapter 9 of the TSD.)

19. DOE requests comment on DOE's methodology to correlate housing starts with hearth products shipments. In addition, DOE requests comment on the assumed three-to-one ratio between non-HPBA and HPBA shipments used to develop the total patio heater shipments assumptions. DOE also requests comment on the assumed fraction of match-lit shipments for each hearth product group and the use of the midpoint of the HPBA range as representative of the market shares of match lit units for each product group as represented in Table 9.3.2 of the TSD. DOE also requests comment on the assumed 0.754 ratio of housing starts to hearth products shipments as discussed in section 9.5 of the TSD and what percentage of these hearth products are connected to natural gas pipelines versus homeowners' propane storage tanks. (See section IV.G and chapter 9 of the TSD.)

20. DOE requests comment on expected industry capital and product conversion costs. For the capital conversion costs, DOE requests comment on the determination that the design standard would primarily entail a component swap, in which manufacturers would assemble hearth products using a different set of purchased parts for the ignition system and that re-tooling or reconfiguring production facilities likely would be limited. In particular, DOE requests comment on the assigned nominal

capital conversion cost per manufacturer, equivalent to $10,000, to account for any one-time capital investments and calculated industry conversion costs of $0.9 million as discussed in Chapter 12.4.6 of the TSD. For the product conversion costs, DOE requests comment on the conversion cost estimates on the assumption that manufacturers would incur limited costs related to R&D, testing and certification, and development of marketing materials in order to bring into compliance models not currently offered with the option of an electronic ignition system. In particular, DOE requests comment on the assumed product conversion cost of $10,000 in fixed costs per model to arrive at the total industry product conversion costs of $7.8 million. DOE also requests comment on the number of hearth product manufacturers who may need to invest in capital equipment, assumed to be 90 manufacturers, and the number of hearth product models, assumed to be 781 models, that may need model redesigns in order to comply with the proposed standards. (See section V.B.2 and chapter 12 of the TSD.)

21. DOE requests comment on potential impacts of an energy conservation standard on domestic production employment. (See section V.B.2 and chapter 12 of the TSD.)

22. DOE requests comment on product-specific regulations that take effect between 2018 and 2024 that would contribute to manufacturers' cumulative regulatory burden. DOE requests information identifying the

specific regulations, as well as data quantifying the associated cost burden

on manufacturers. (See section V.B.2 and chapter 12 of the TSD.)

23. DOE requests comment on the approach for estimating monetary benefits

associated with emissions reductions. (See section V.B.6 and chapter 14

of the TSD.)

www.ingramcontent.com/pod-product-compliance
Lightning Source LLC
Chambersburg PA
CBHW080247290526

45790CB00005B/1732